Troy Guy gives a thoughtf
his reasons for faith in th
proach is systematic and well documented.

Dr. Steven J. Meyer, S.T.L., S.T.D.
Assistant Professor of Theology
University of St. Thomas School of Theology
Houston, Texas

An engineer is by nature a curious person—someone who likes to figure things out and who can take a complex idea and make it simple and workable. Engineer, Troy Guy, has done just that in his precise analysis of the Catholic Church. As if with his exacting micrometer in hand, Troy has measured all contenders for the "pillar and foundation of the truth" and has discovered that God the Eternal Engineer has designed but one structure that will stand the test of time until her Master Builder returns. They say that "simplicity is a mark of genius" and "the less parts the better" so with that in mind I'd like to say THANK YOU, Troy, for giving us such a genius tour de force of your faith journey and making the complex simple!

John D. Lewis, ATP, CFI
Professional Worldwide Gulfstream Pilot, Hong Kong
Author of *Caravan: Cessna's Swiss Army Knife with Wings*

Evangelical Catholic is one of the best books on Catholic apologetics I have ever read! It is scripturally based, deeply rooted in Church tradition, and portrays the "freshness" of Troy's recent discernment and passionate conversion. It will be useful for Catholics who are deepening and defending their faith, as well as, Protestants seeking the truth.

Deacon Scott Daniel
St. Paul the Apostle Catholic Church
Nassau Bay, Texas

I found myself church hopping as I searched for answers to questions that are simply unanswerable in Protestantism. *Evangelical Catholic* is a scripturally based masterpiece that answered my questions with clarity and precision. This book brought me closer to Christ and His Church. I highly recommend it for any Protestant or Catholic wishing to strengthen their faith!

Sarah Mills
Former Evangelical Protestant
Austin, Texas

Great contributions to Catholic apologetics have been made by converts. *Evangelical Catholic* by Troy Guy is one such work. One of its strengths is the historical record that he presents: the writings of the early Church affirm the 2,000-year teachings of the Catholic Church. They are in fact that which was handed down by the apostles. This book will be a valuable asset in RCIA. Gold star here!

Rich May
BA, MA Theology
Houston, TX

EVANGELICAL CATHOLIC

A journey through the Biblical and historical evidence that led *yet another* evangelical Protestant to the Apostolic Church!

Troy L. Guy

LEONINE PUBLISHERS
PHOENIX, ARIZONA

Printed with ecclesiastical permission

✠ Cardinal Daniel N. DiNardo
Archbishop of Galveston-Houston
October 25, 2017

The *Nihil obstat* and *Imprimatur* are official declarations that a book or pamphlet is free from doctrinal or moral error. No implication is contained therein that those who have granted the *Nihil obstat* and *Imprimatur* agree with the contents, opinions, or statements expressed.

Published by

Leonine Publishers LLC
Phoenix, Arizona, USA

ISBN-13: 978-1-942190-39-4
Library of Congress Control Number: 2017957931

Printed in the United States of America
10 9 8 7 6 5 4 3 2 1

Visit us online at www.leoninepublishers.com
For more information: info@leoninepublishers.com

Contents

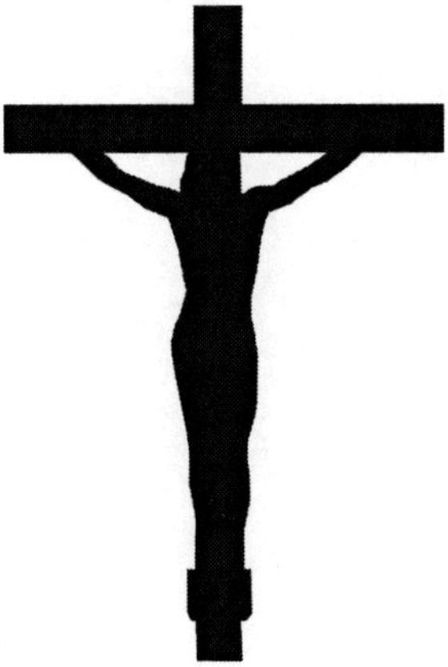

So that all of them may be one.

Introduction

After twenty-five years as an evangelical Protestant Christian (Baptist and non-denominational), I discovered that the Catholic Church *is* the Church that Jesus established 2,000 years ago. Jesus established a visible Church which is One, Holy, Catholic, and Apostolic. The Catholic Church has an unbroken line of apostolic succession traceable directly back to the Apostle Peter, and therefore, to Jesus Christ our Lord! It is within the Catholic Church that sacred mysteries are forever proclaimed and the Holy Eucharist, instituted by Christ, is experienced.

Why did I convert to Catholic Christianity? What on earth would thrust someone to leave their vibrant evangelical church to become a Catholic Christian? I asked these questions of converts before I arrived at a similar point in faith. In an attempt to provide an answer, allow me to borrow a line from G.K. Chesterton, an Anglican convert to Catholicism himself:

> The difficulty of explaining "why I am a Catholic" is that there are ten thousand reasons all amounting to one reason: that Catholicism is true.[1]

---

[1] G.K. Chesterton, "Why I Am a Catholic," from Twelve Modern Apostles and Their Creeds (1926).

Chesterton's words certainly apply to any attempt to fully quantify the uncontainable beauty and truth found in the Catholic Church. There is another reality at work that prevented me from seeing these riches sooner. Archbishop Fulton J. Sheen said it this way:

> There are not over a hundred people in the United States who hate the Catholic Church. There are millions, however, who hate what they wrongly believe to be the Catholic Church.[2]

Over time a cascade of persistent inconsistencies and historical deficiencies within Protestantism became clear, which forced me to inescapable conclusions. John Henry Newman, who like G.K. Chesterton was an Anglican convert to Catholicism, echoed my own surprising experience:

> To be deep in history is to cease to be Protestant.[3]

Biblical and historical evidence, coupled with intellectual honesty, compelled my conversion.

In Praise of Non-Catholic Christians!

I accepted Jesus as my Lord and Savior and was baptized in July of 1989. I am deeply grateful for my evangelical Christian heritage. It ignited a genuine passion for following Christ in my life. I have experienced spiritual growth through the preaching and

---

[2] Leslie Rumble, *Radio Replies*, First Volume (Charlotte, NC: TAN Books, 2012), ix.

[3] John Henry Newman (1801-1890).

teaching of many faithful evangelical pastors. There is no doubt that the Holy Spirit works within Protestant Christianity in remarkable ways. My experience in the Baptist church has proved fruitful in my spiritual journey. Many of my closest friends remain faithful within Protestant Christianity and my love for all of them continues without restriction! They are my brothers and sisters in Christ! Our principal purpose in life is to know, love, and follow Jesus. This, I submit, holds us together even when disagreements arise. "By this everyone will know that you are my disciples, if you love one another" (John 13:35).

"But what about…?"

I am certain you have heard these claims or questions: Why convert to the Catholic faith over the Episcopal, Anglican, or Orthodox traditions? Why do Catholics worship Mary? Why do Catholics pray to dead saints? Why do Catholic churches have statues, sacred images, icons, candles, and other types of aids when the Bible condemns the worship of graven images? Is the Lord's Supper only symbolic? Isn't the Catholic Church boring, irrelevant, and ritualistic? Isn't church a group of like-minded believers who gather together to pray, read the Bible, sing, and fellowship; so, why do we need any church? Why do Catholics follow man-made traditions? Who needs a pope when we have Jesus and the Bible? Is *sola scriptura*, also known as the "Bible alone" theory, Biblical? Did the faith of the first Christians and early Church Fathers reflect modern Protestant teachings?

My heartfelt prayer is that this book will guide you to understand the Catholic faith and fall in love with it as I did. Perhaps you will consider "coming home" to Catholic Christianity and growing closer to Jesus through the one Church He established.

God bless your journey!

Troy L. Guy

Chapter 1

Not Called to Entertainment

Enter, let us bow down in worship;
let us kneel before the LORD who made us.
(Psalms 95:6)

God alone can satisfy the human soul. To experience God intimately, we must worship Him in "spirit and in truth" (John 4:24). How can we worship God in *truth*? What does authentic worship look like? Joseph Cardinal Ratzinger captures an important observation in the search for authentic worship:

> Man himself cannot simply "make" worship. If God does not reveal himself, man is clutching empty space… But real liturgy implies that God responds and reveals how we can worship him… It cannot spring from imagination, our own creativity—then it would remain just a cry in the dark or mere self-affirmation. Liturgy implies a real relationship with Another, who reveals himself to us and gives our existence a new direction.[4]

---

[4] Joseph Cardinal Ratzinger, *The Spirit of the Liturgy* (San Francisco, CA: Ignatius Press, 2000), 21-22.

Church Shopping and Consumerism

I observed, through many years in Christian ministry, a strong resemblance between Protestant churches and American consumerism. Selecting a church essentially boiled down to finding the right combination of "personal choices" and "individual preferences" on an unending menu. Passionate preaching, upbeat music, the most innovative children's ministry, social activities, home groups, and so on, typically defined the acceptability of one Protestant church over another Protestant church. In other words, shopping for churches was like shopping for anything else! Any church that closely matched one's own standards and stipulations was a potential church home effectively creating a church "in one's own image." The choice-driven, market-based consumerism I experienced in Protestant churches felt like a rivalry for members rather than a quest for Christian unity. I found it impossible to nail down exactly what evangelical Protestantism stood for through the overabundance of choices, offerings, and comforts. Should finding the Church Jesus established be equivalent to shopping for whatever satisfies our desires? Is the Protestant church movement, to attract members by creating enticing opportunities, what God intended for His Church?

In America, church shopping is the norm, where "not being fed" is frequently cited as the motivation for leaving one church for another. Their particular church experience or expectations simply were not met. Writing about Protestant consumerism, Devin Rose observes:

> This mentality fits into our Western culture's consumeristic idea that we should have multiple choices for everything. Why should I go to a Church that "I don't get anything out of?" I don't willingly subject myself to inconvenience and pain in other areas of my life, so why do it on Sundays? I want a Church that fits my tastes, plays worship music I like, has people of the same age and demographic as me, provides activities that I find meaningful, and teaches articles of faith and morals that make me feel good about what I already believe and do... At the heart of Protestantism's ecclesial consumerism is an assumption that there is no one true, visible Church ... The Catholic understanding is the opposite. There is a visible Church that Christ established, but Protestant communities have broken off in schism from it.[5]

Perhaps man-made aspects of Protestantism are the true culprit behind the consumeristic "church hopping" we observe so clearly today, which nag at the hearts of those who seek to know, love, and follow Jesus. If we do not find authentic worship, established by God, then all "that is left in the end is frustration, a feeling of emptiness."[6] Church hopping soon sets in. This is the experience for many evangelical Protestants; I was no exception!

---

[5] Devin Rose, *The Protestant's Dilemma* (San Diego, CA: Catholic Answers Press, 2014), 188-189.

[6] Ratzinger, 23.

> How often do we convince ourselves that the music will be better at *that* church, the sermons more exciting when preached by *that* pastor, or our spiritual hunger will be satisfied by *that* group, church, movement, book, tape, prophet, leader, speaker, or televangelist?[7]

Evangelical Protestant worship "services" are designed to deliver Biblical truth through practical, dynamic, engaging, and family-friendly sermons. These innovations are helpful, but the *fullness of truth* cannot be experienced in this way. Despite the best efforts of contemporary evangelicalism to create vibrant and entertaining worship services, my soul continued to yearn for deeper interactions with God. Church shopping based on our feelings and expectations seemed at odds to what the early Church experienced. Further, the Bible only speaks of the *one* Church Jesus established in Matthew 16:18 not thousands of self-defined denominations. Christ prayed for Christian unity in John 17:20-23!

Who Decides for *You*?

In evangelical Protestantism, the pastor *individually* decides what the congregation will hear based on what they "feel led" to preach. A pastor challenged with finances may develop his sermons toward stewardship. Another pastor, convinced God is calling him to expand the church, may preach on giving. Still a

---

[7] Jeff Cavins, *"I'm Not Being Fed!"* (West Chester, PA: Ascension Press, 2005), 2.

different pastor, trained at a Bible college founded on reformer John Calvin, will preach on Calvinism and predestination. One Christmas, our family visited a Methodist church where the pastor preached for over an hour on the theology of John Wesley. This Protestant pastor deeply believed he was "called" to preach the gospel as understood by Wesley. The list goes on. On the Protestant plan, people living within ten square miles of each other hear vastly different sermons and teachings which are each selected based on a particular pastor's druthers. In this way, evangelical pastors "feed" their flock.

Sitting in a Baptist church one morning, questions began nagging me like a persistent fly: By what *authority* do Protestant pastors preach? Am I really being fed what God intended? Is this truth or am I receiving an imitation? My heart became stirred when trying to make sense of over 30,000 Protestant denominations (Center for the Study of Global Christianity, Gordon-Conwell Theological Seminary, June 2013) each teaching their own version of truth. I knew, at this point, something was deeply wrong.

A Heart for More!

"You have made us for yourself, O Lord, and our heart is restless until it rests in you."
Augustine, Bishop of Hippo (AD 354-430)

What a beautiful truth! Augustine points out that our hearts will be stirred until we find God, and worship Him *the way* He intended. Indeed, as Augustine said, my heart became restless over the years as my soul became dry on what I experienced to be *pastor*-centric, *consumeristic,* and *entertaining* worship "services." Yet, through extensive study of the Bible and the early Church Fathers, it became clear that the early Church worshipped God much differently! In fact, the very *center* of worship was not a pastor! It was not the music! It was not solely the message! In the following chapters, we will encounter Christ and discover *the one Church He established.* Indeed, we are called to experience Someone much greater than entertainment!

Chapter 2

Encountering Jesus of Nazareth

God demonstrates his own love for us in this:
While we were still sinners, Christ died for us.
(Romans 5:8)

Authentic Christian faith is a transforming encounter with a Person: Jesus of Nazareth. The Christian faith is not solely focused on learning and knowing facts, although they are important and necessary. Christianity is not merely a set of beliefs based on ethics or intellectual superiority, however important they are. It is more than a mental assent and acknowledgment of historical truths, but understanding history is incredibly vital. The Christian faith is also an experience and relationship with God. To walk with Him personally, now and for eternity, is the Christian life.

We Are His Creation

God created everything, both the observable and unobservable. God created man and woman in His image, which from the very beginning were intended to be in union with Him, in a pure and right relationship. We were created to walk side by side in His holy presence and enjoy all of His creation to the fullest. Our hearts are formed to be oriented toward Him as our loving Father, our first love, and intimate friend. God was well pleased when He created us. God said that His creation was "very good."[8] Man and woman, then, were created as the very apple of God's eye.

A Path Not Chosen by God

Man took a different path than God intended. Since the creation of time, rebellion and disobedience have placed a stain on the very heart of the human soul leading to separation from God. Satan, along with his fallen angels, has opposed God and all God created from the beginning of time. Man and woman were enticed by the apparent goodness offered by Satan. This choice created separation between God and man. The horrible consequence of selecting that which is not of God is called sin and it leads precisely to our spiritual and physical death. Sin sets itself against God's love for us and turns our hearts away from it. Like the first sin, it is disobedience, a revolt against God through the will to become "like gods" knowing and determining good and evil. Sin is thus "love of oneself even to contempt of God."[9] The impacts are clear and can be observed today through greed, war, hate, fighting, hypocrisy, pain, death, lust, envy, lying, poverty, prejudice, and a multitude of other anomalies. Our relationship with Him has suffered, as well as our relationships with one another.

Mercy and Love

Despite our failures and attempts to replace His love with counterfeits, God continues to have perfect love

[8] Genesis 1:31.

[9] *Catechism of the Catholic Church* (CCC), n. 1850.

for all people. He has never stopped seeking an intimate, intentional, and personal relationship with the sinner. Sacred Scripture describes an unfathomable act performed by God to save us from our destructive and sinful behavior. God became man, so that, He could free us given that we could not free ourselves. God in flesh, Jesus of Nazareth, took our sins upon Himself and was crucified in cold blood for the public to see. This is the love of God.

Salvation Has Come!

The story, if it ended there, would be the end of Christianity. Yet, an earth-shattering event took place in history that literally changed the world and all of creation. On the third day after being unjustly crucified, Jesus Christ rose from the dead. Paul provides a concise observation of the Gospel of Christ:

> For I handed on to you as of first importance what I also received: that Christ died for our sins in accordance with the Scriptures; that he was buried; that he was raised on the third day in accordance with the Scriptures; that he appeared to Cephas, then to the Twelve. After that, he appeared to more than five hundred brothers at once... After that he appeared to James, then to all the apostles (1 Corinthians 15:3-7).

Christ, and His resurrection from the dead, now gives tangible *hope* to the entire world! God became man so that He could stand for us and obtain eternal sacrifice and salvation. Only God can satisfy the demands of what our sin called for. A personal relationship with Jesus Christ is required for salvation. Peter calls everyone to enter into this personal relationship with God by repenting of our sins, authentically placing our faith in Jesus Christ as our Savior, and sacrificially following Christ in being baptized:

> Repent and be baptized, every one of you, in the name of Jesus Christ for the forgiveness of your sins, and you will receive the gift of the Holy Spirit. For the promise is made to you and to your children and to all those far off, whomever the Lord our God will call (Acts of the Apostles 2:38-39).

Jesus said that He is the way to heaven and calls everyone to believe and follow Him. Like the disciples before us, we are asked if we believe this:

> I am the resurrection and the life; whoever believes in me, even if he dies, will live, and everyone who lives and believes in me will never die. Do you believe this? (John 11:25-26).

Jesus conquered death, so that all who believe in Him, repent of their sin, and trust in Him fully are able to come back to God and live in eternity with Him. This is the "Good News!"

> For God so loved the world that he gave his only Son, so that everyone who believes in him might not perish but might have eternal life (John 3:16).

Knowing Jesus Christ personally is an invitation open to everyone. As with any gift, we must choose to open and receive it. To follow Christ, or not to follow Him, demands a response from each of us. Have you opened this gift God has offered you? Do you know Jesus *personally*?

Chapter 3

The Nicene Creed: Early Christian Profession of Faith

To him be glory in the Church and in Christ Jesus to all generations, forever and ever. Amen.
(Ephesians 3:21)

The first disciples of Jesus were commissioned "to make disciples of all nations, baptizing them in the name of the Father, and of the Son, and of the Holy Spirit" (Matthew 28:19). They were sent to spread the salvation message of Jesus to every person and nation with great boldness through the Holy Spirit (Acts of the Apostles 2). Their hearts were set ablaze and filled with power and fire from heaven. Christianity miraculously spread throughout large parts of the region.

For the first 300 years after Christ, the Church suffered persecution and attacks both spiritually and physically. Periodic persecutions and acts of violence against Christians continued from the time of the apostles until Emperor Constantine.

With the Edict of Milan in AD 313, tolerance of Christianity was instituted throughout the empire. At this point in history, persecutions against Christians largely subsided. Of course, history shows persecution of Christians would return. For the time being, legal protection of Christianity allowed growth of the Church in the public square. With open freedom to worship now at hand, the rise of heresy (beliefs *contrary* to orthodox faith which was handed down directly from Christ to the apostles) also began to sprout.

The young Church went from fighting persecution to fighting theological heresy and doctrinal errors spread by various groups. Thus, the Church formed councils to guard the faith and affirm truth that had been handed down from the apostles. Jesus established His Church and promised that the "gates of hell would not prevail against it" (Matthew 16:18) and the early Church councils aided in that protection through the guidance and direction of the Holy Spirit.

The Council at Jerusalem

Converted Pharisees from Jerusalem were promoting that Gentile Christians should be required to observe Mosaic Law, specifically relating to the requirement of circumcision. This group advocated that "unless you are circumcised according to the Mosaic practice you cannot be saved" (Acts of the Apostles 15:1). Thus, the Council of Jerusalem was formed in AD 49 to consider this issue disturbing the Church. The Jerusalem Council *authoritatively* determined that Gentile Christians were not required to follow the Mosaic Law and issued a formally binding decision on behalf of the entire Christian Church: "It is the decision of the Holy Spirit *and of us* not to place on you any burden beyond these necessities" (Acts of the Apostles 15:28). The importance for our consideration is twofold. First, recognize that an *infallible judgment* was made by the Church through the Holy Spirit at the Council of Jerusalem, which is accepted as binding by all Christians and still believed today. Second, the early Church had *divine authority* to make these infallible decisions relating to matters of faith and morals *before* the New Testament was finally complete. Notice they did *not* have a completed New Testament, but they *did* have a living and authoritative Church established by Christ to make this decision for all Christians.

The Nicene Creed

Christians believe Jesus is fully human and fully God. This is a central mystery of the Christian faith and considered orthodox in all Christian traditions. However, there were non-orthodox views that began circulating in the early Church. A priest, Arius of Alexandria, began teaching Jesus was not divine. In his view, Jesus is a created creature, not the eternal Creator.

The First Council of Nicaea was held in AD 325 to respond to this growing Arian heresy. At this council, bishops authoritatively affirmed Jesus is divine, not created. A statement of faith was developed that confirmed Jesus to be "of the same substance" or "one in being" with the Father.

The creed developed at Nicaea was later amended at the Council of Constantinople in AD 381, to include the Divinity of the Holy Spirit. The profession of faith Christians recite today is this creed passed down from the bishops at Constantinople:

> I believe in one God, the Father almighty, maker of heaven and earth, of all things visible and invisible.

I believe in one Lord Jesus Christ, the Only Begotten Son of God, born of the Father before all ages. God from God, Light from Light, true God from true God, begotten, not made, consubstantial with the Father; through Him all things were made.

For us men and for our salvation He came down from heaven, and by the Holy Spirit was incarnate of the Virgin Mary, and became man.

For our sake He was crucified under Pontius Pilate, He suffered death and was buried, and rose again on the third day in accordance with the Scriptures.

He ascended into heaven and is seated at the right hand of the Father. He will come again in glory to judge the living and the dead and his kingdom will have no end.

I believe in the Holy Spirit, the Lord, the giver of life, who proceeds from the Father and the Son, who with the Father and the Son is adored and glorified, who has spoken through the prophets.

I believe in **one, holy, catholic, and apostolic Church.** I confess one baptism for the forgiveness of sins and I look forward to the resurrection of the dead and the life of the world to come. Amen.

The Four Marks of the Church

One line in the Nicene Creed caused an avalanche of ecclesiological (study of Church) and theological concerns within my evangelical stronghold: "I believe in *one, holy, catholic,* and *apostolic* Church." These four marks of the Church were identified as essential points in defining the true Church. As an evangelical Protestant, I faithfully acknowledged the words of the Nicene Creed, reciting it word for word, but living the implications of their *meaning* was a bit more disturbing.

"Can I make the same claim about my church?"

How could I sincerely say that my Baptist church was *one*? In Protestantism there is not *one*, but literally thousands of different denominations each claiming divine truth. In fact, there are over 30,000 different Protestant denominations, including "non-denominational" denominations! How could I harmonize these vast divisions in Protestantism with the call to be *one* Church?

Likewise, how could I claim my church was "catholic" (e.g., universal) in any true historical sense before AD 1500? There was not a single Protestant church in *existence* prior to AD 1517! Being catholic implies that my Protestant church had to have *existed* from the time of Christ and sent missionaries throughout the world in the first, second, third, fourth, fifth, and following centuries leading up to the Protestant Reformation.

Further, my evangelical Protestant church could not have been *apostolic* since it was *founded* over 1,500 years *after* Christ promised to establish His Church on earth. Even the most extravagant explanation offers no solution to the problem of Protestantism's lack of apostolic history.

> This is the sole Church of Christ, which in the Creed we profess to be one, holy, catholic, and apostolic. These four characteristics, inseparably linked with each other, indicate essential features of the Church and her mission. The Church does not possess them of herself; it is Christ who, through the Holy Spirit, makes his Church one, holy, catholic, and apostolic, and it is he who calls her to realize each of these qualities.[10]

What exactly happened during the 1,500 year period between Christ establishing His Church (Matthew 16:18) with the promise that the gates of hell would *never* prevail against it *until* the Protestant Reformation?

Were millions of people living during that time left without a true Church? To the contrary! Biblical and historical evidence leaves no doubt that Jesus never abandoned His Church! Through a precise examination of the four marks in the Nicene Creed, the one and only Church Jesus established emerges with striking clarity.

[10] CCC, n. 811.

Chapter 4

One, Holy, Catholic, and Apostolic Church

God's household, which is the Church of the living God the pillar and foundation of the truth.
(1 Timothy 3:15)

✟ What I **discovered** …

The four marks of the early Church, captured in the Nicene Creed (one, holy, catholic, apostolic), demonstrate that the Catholic Church is in fact the Church Jesus established 2,000 years ago. Biblical, historical, logical, and practical evidence for this finding is certain and exhaustive.

~ 📖 ~

Fr. Francis J. Ripley captures an appropriate prelude for this chapter:

> The plain fact is that if we go back through history, looking for the Church **personally established by Christ**, we find that all the non-Catholic bodies disappear at various times subsequent to the death of Christ. Only the Catholic Church endures in a search back through history. The others claim Christ as their head, but they admit some man as their founder; **the Catholic Church alone claims Christ as both its**

> **Founder and its Head.** And not only does she *claim* divine foundation, she clearly *proves* that claim. The only valid conclusion you can draw from this instruction is that Christ, who is God, founded a visible, organized Church and promised that it would last until the End of Time. Therefore, that visible, organized Church is in the world today. It can be identified by its four marks, imprinted on it by Christ: 1) miraculous unity, 2) universality, 3) outstanding holiness, and 4) unbroken Apostolic descent. No denomination can be Christ's Church unless it possesses those four marks. The Catholic Church alone possesses them...[11] [emphasis added].

We now turn our attention to these essential marks (one, holy, catholic, apostolic) of the Church.

The First Mark of the Original Church: The Church Is *One*

Jesus established *one* Church. He is our one Shepherd and we are His one flock. Jesus said that His people will hear His voice and follow Him.

> I have other sheep that do not belong to this fold. These also I must lead, and they will hear my voice, and there will be **one flock**, one shepherd (John 10:16).

[11] Canon Francis Ripley, *This Is the Faith* (Rockford, IL: TAN Books, 2002), 149-150.

Jesus specifically prayed for the unity of *all* Christians. In John's Gospel, when praying for the disciples and their mission, Jesus prayed that they would be one. The weight given to His desire for *unity* is compared to none other than the Holy Trinity, Who is *one* God!

> My prayer is not for them alone. I pray also for those who will believe in me through their message, that **all of them may be one**, Father, just as you are in me and I am in you. May they also be in us so that the world may believe that you have sent me (John 17:20-21).

Scripture tells us that there is *one* Bride of Christ, the Church. Paul compares the Church to the special relationship a husband has with his wife. The Biblical covenant of marriage is an intimate union reflective of His mystical unification with the *one* Church He established.

> Husbands, love your wives, just as Christ loved **the church** and gave Himself up for her to make her holy, cleansing her by the washing with water through the word, and to present her to Himself as **a radiant church**, without stain or wrinkle or any other blemish, but holy and blameless (Ephesians 5:25-27).

I recall my wedding in 2001. As my beautiful bride was slowly being escorted toward the altar, my heart jumped and filled with unimaginable joy, knowing that I would become *one* with her! She is one person, not many, and I was overwhelmed at just how special this union is. The Bible only knows of *one* Church, "a radiant Church." How must God feel when we bring Him multiple churches, separated and broken, in what is supposed to be a divine union with His Bride, the Church?

Paul insists the Church agree, have no divisions, and be united. He follows his exhortation concerning dissention in the Church with a question that seems to almost pretentiously and prophetically challenge Protestant denominational divisions today.

> I appeal to you, brothers and sisters, in the name of our Lord Jesus Christ, that all of you **agree with one another** in what you say and that there be **no divisions** among you, but that you be **perfectly united** in mind and thought. **Is Christ divided**...? (1 Corinthians 1:10, 13).

Paul says that Christians are one body, have one faith, and participate in one baptism. We are united with Christ and united with each other through Christ our Lord.

> Because there is one bread, we who are many are **one body**, for we all partake of the one bread (1 Corinthians 10:17).

> There is **one** body and **one** Spirit, just as you were called to the **one** hope that belongs to your call, **one** Lord, **one** faith, **one** baptism, **one** God and Father of us all, who is above all and through all and in all (Ephesians 4:4-6).

Disunity—The Protestant Reformation

Since the Protestant Reformation in AD 1517, when the German Augustinian monk Martin Luther nailed his 95 Theses on the door of the Wittenberg Castle Church, there have been thousands upon thousands of different Protestant denominations formed. The Catholic Church needed reform but the idea that Christ allowed His Church to decline into unrecoverable destruction for over 1,000 years is a theory not grounded in either Biblical or historical fact. Regardless, the impact of Martin Luther's Reformation agenda unleashed a devastating blow to the unity of the Christian Church that continues to divide and split today. A listing, albeit not exhaustive, of Protestant tradition origins is instructive. Note that before Martin Luther started the Reformation, there were no Protestant denominations.

When was *your* church founded?

Church	**Founder**	**Date**
Catholic Church	Jesus Christ	AD 33
↓	No Protestant churches for over **1,500 years!**	↓
Lutheran	Martin Luther	AD 1517
Calvinist	John Calvin	AD 1555
Presbyterian	John Knox	AD 1560
Baptist	John Smyth	AD 1609
Quakers	George Fox	AD 1649
Amish	Jacob Amman	AD 1693
Methodist	John and Charles Wesley	AD 1739

Episcopal	Samuel Seabury	AD 1789
Disciples of Christ	Thomas Campbell	AD 1827
Churches of Christ	Warren Stone	AD 1836
Seventh-day Adventist	Ellen White	AD 1844
Pentecostal	Charles Parkham	AD 1901
Assemblies of God	from Pentecostals	AD 1914
Foursquare Gospel	Aimee Semple	AD 1917
Calvary Chapel	Chuck Smith	AD 1965
Vineyard	Kenn Gulliksen	AD 1974
Saddleback	Rick Warren	AD 1982
Non-denominational	anyone	weekly

Seeing *Cracks* in the Foundation of Protestantism

As my studies went on, important historical and theological questions arising from the time of the Reformation became uncomfortable and unanswerable. For example, did the Church founded by Christ in AD 33 cease to exist until Martin Luther was born; the same Church that Christ promised hell would *never* prevail against? To believe this seems to bring our Lord's promise into question. Was the Church left without the Holy Spirit for over 1,400 years, despite Jesus promising to send the Holy Spirit to guide and protect it? (John 14:26 and 16:13, Acts of the Apostles 15:27-28). Does it make sense that every time a Protestant becomes disheartened he should leave his current church and start a new church or denomination that he feels "called" to start? The visible fruits of division created since the Protestant Reformation produces an extremely frail position for the sincere Protestant studying Christian history.

Protestant denominations ultimately find their origins in man: *Martin Luther* (Lutheran church), *King Henry VIII* (Church of England), *John Knox* (Presbyterian church), *John Smyth* (Baptist church), *John Wesley* (Methodist church), *Thomas Campbell* (Disciples of Christ church), *Chuck Smith* (Calvary Chapel), *Bill Hybels* (Willow Creek movement), *George Fox* (Quakers), *Phineas Bresee* (Church of the Nazarene), *Charles Harrison Mason* (Church of God in Christ), *Charles Parham* (Assemblies of God), *Aimee McPherson* (Foursquare Gospel), *Kenn Gulliksen* (Vineyard church), *Loren Cunningham* (Youth With A Mission), Bill Bright (Campus Crusade for Christ) and so on. What man can be named as founder for the apostolic Christian Church? The implication, for me, was eye-opening!

The Church of England was formed out of King Henry VIII's desire to divorce his first wife, Catherine of Aragon. When Pope Clement VII declined his request for an annulment, King Henry VIII broke with the Catholic Church to begin the Church of England.[12] Interestingly, King Henry VIII would eventually have not two, but six wives. Two of his wives were executed by beheading. Two others he divorced. Even though King Henry VIII broke with the Catholic Church formally and became a self-appointed authority, he maintained many Catholic theological underpinnings and ideas. Further splitting occurred as the Anglican and Episcopal churches would later develop from the

[12] John Vidmar, *The Catholic Church Through the Ages: A History* (Mahwah, NJ: Paulist Press, 2014), 212-218.

Church of England. Did one man's desire for divorce truly justify breaking from the *one* Church Christ established?

One historical fact is certain: *all* Protestant churches, despite their individualized reasons, broke off from the apostolic Church with the poignant consequences of creating division and denominational chaos throughout Christianity.

"We disagree only on the small things"

I recall asking my Baptist pastor why there were so many different Protestant churches. He reassured me, "We agree on the major things. We simply disagree on the minor details of our faith. Basically, in essentials we have unity, in non-essentials we exercise liberty, and in all things we practice charity." His well-meaning answer generated a more probing question in my mind. After all, where in the Bible do we find an authoritative list of what the "major" or "minor" issues are? Minor articles of faith in one Protestant church are often *major* doctrines in a different Protestant church, and vice versa. How can these differences in what constitutes "major" or "minor" doctrine ever be reconciled within Protestantism? For example, there is always grave disunity in the following areas:

Baptism: Presbyterians, Lutherans, and Methodists are certain the Bible teaches infant baptism. Yet, for Baptist and fundamentalist Bible churches, only professing adults may be baptized. Further, some Protestants teach that baptism is required for salvation while other Protestants teach baptism is only a symbol. Christ commands His followers to be baptized (Matthew 28:19-20, Mark 16:16). Apostle Peter calls us to follow Christ in baptism (1 Peter 3:21). If baptism is important to Christ and the early Church, it must be a major issue—not an optional doctrine left to the discretion of individual Protestant churches.

Salvation: Are Christians saved through faith *alone*? Can Christians lose their salvation? Is this a major issue? Many evangelical denominations are strongly divided on salvation.

Gifts of the Holy Spirit: Some fundamentalist Protestant churches teach that divinely appointed gifts of the Holy Spirit, such as speaking in tongues and physical healing, have ceased. According to them, spiritual gifts were used for a purpose but then taken away soon after the Church began. Other Protestant churches fully accept and earnestly invite the spiritual gifts. Isn't healing, a concern of Christ, a major issue? Isn't healing something we are told to pray for with expectancy? In fact, aren't all the spiritual gifts fruitful for the Christian life major issues?

Sanctity of Life: The unborn are caught up in the social war over pro-choice or pro-life ideologies. Sadly, the only person *without a choice* is the baby. What protection does a baby have? In some Protestant churches, pro-choice seems like the answer. In other Protestant churches, there is unity against the death of a child whether inside the womb or out. Life begins at conception. The heartbeat begins just 18 days after. Isn't human life, the very gift of God, a major issue? (Exodus 20:13, Proverbs 6:16-17, Psalms 127:3, Jeremiah 1:5).

Did you know that before 1930 *all* Christian churches taught that abortion and contraception were evil?

The Lambeth Conference, a group of Anglican bishops summoned by the Archbishop of Canterbury in 1930, decided that Holy Matrimony and procreation could include *denial of birth* through contraception. The Anglican church was the first to break away from this long-held Christian doctrine rooted in Scripture, Tradition, and natural moral law. This decision radically departed from almost 2,000 years of Christian doctrine! Sadly, the majority of other Protestant denominations quickly fell down the same slippery slope. Abortion and contraception are evils that *all* Christian churches just a few generations ago condemned! Today, however, only the Catholic Church continues to sail steadfast against the stormy, unstable sea of moral relativism—a testament that the Catholic Church is guided by the Spirit of Truth in its fullness.

Should the elderly be assisted in dying? Some Protestant traditions believe life is to end naturally. Others advocate euthanasia as a solution to solve end-of-life issues, pain, suffering, and financial burden. Is the life of our grandparents a theological or moral issue? Surely, contraception, abortion, and euthanasia are major moral issues?

Clergy: Some Protestant denominations allow, and encourage, those with same-sex attraction to lead their church. Other Protestant denominations respect the rights of those who have same-sex attraction, but do not allow them to lead their particular church. Is this a major issue?

Division Creates Logical Chaos

Suppose Protestant minister A, claiming to be filled with the Holy Spirit, asserts he is teaching truth about doctrine Y (e.g., salvation is by faith *alone*). Protestant minister B, also claiming to be filled with the Holy Spirit, asserts his interpretation of Y is the truth (e.g., salvation is by faith *and* works). Is not one of the two pastors absolutely in error about Y? If so, one of these Protestant congregations would not be receiving the *fullness of truth* at best, or receiving *error* at the worst!

As a Protestant Christian, this dilemma created a theological wrestling match within my soul. Thousands of different Protestant churches and leaders claim to be led by the Holy Spirit and follow the "Bible alone" as their only source of divine authority. Yet, how could such vast divisions occur if they are truly following what they "hear from God?" I knew this dilemma boiled down to *authority*, but just how this authority manifested itself in Protestant Christianity become more and more ambiguous, distant, and unsettling!

The authority to resolve these questions of faith *never* demands an answer in the Protestant framework. One may simply join a different Protestant church that supports what the "Holy Spirit is telling them." Yet, the Holy Spirit will not give contradictory or false teaching!

There is no *divinely* established authority in the more than 30,000 different Protestant denominations linking them back to the apostolic Church established by Jesus in Matthew 16:17-19.

A kind of free-for-all has set in. Protestantism is unable—Biblically, historically, or logically—to be characterized as *one* Church!

The Second Mark of the Original Church: The Church is *Holy*

The Church is a hospital for sinners, not a museum of saints! The Church is not holy because of her inherent goodness, but rather the perfection and holiness of her Head.

> "The Church . . . is held, as a matter of faith, to be unfailingly holy. This is because Christ, the Son of God, who with the Father and the Spirit is hailed as 'alone holy,' loved the Church as his Bride, giving himself up for her so as to sanctify her; he joined her to himself as his body and endowed her with the gift of the Holy Spirit for the glory of God." The Church, then, is "the holy People of God," and her members are called "saints."[13]

The Holy Spirit indwells in the members of the Church to clean and sanctify them. The Holy Trinity is actively involved in saving and cleansing the entire body of Christ. In this way, the dark hospital of sinners is transformed into a bright display of saints.

[13] CCC, n. 823.

The Third Mark of the Original Church: The Church is *Catholic*

Catholic means "universal." The Catholic Church includes people from all nations. The disciples were commissioned to go to the ends of the earth to reach all people with the Good News of salvation in Jesus Christ:

> Go, therefore, and make disciples of **all nations**, baptizing them in the name of the Father, and of the Son, and of the Holy Spirit… (Matthew 28:19).
>
> He said to them, "Go into **all the world** and preach the good news to all creation. Whoever believes and is baptized will be saved, but whoever does not believe will be condemned" (Mark 16:15-16).

What Protestant church can legitimately claim "universality" in the period from AD 33 until AD 500? The same question holds from AD 500 to AD 1000. My Baptist church claimed universality in reach, through the sending of missionaries to various countries around the world. But even in the best case, this only demonstrates recent universality (e.g., being "catholic" from AD 1500 to present). Historical evidence pins Protestantism on the horns of a serious predicament. There were no Protestant churches in existence until *after* AD 1500. Thus Protestantism, by definition, can make no claim to be historically universal. Through historical and intellectual honesty, it is easy to see how John Henry Newman's discovery quickly became part of my own story: "To be deep in history is to cease to be Protestant."

The Fourth Mark of the Original Church: The Church is *Apostolic*

The Catholic Church is *apostolic* in that it can prove an unbroken line of apostolic succession traceable directly back to the Apostle Peter, and therefore, to Jesus Christ.

> The Church is apostolic in her *origin* because she has been built on "the foundation of the apostles" (Ephesians 2:20). She is apostolic in her *teaching* which is the same as that of the Apostles. She is apostolic by reason of her *structure* insofar as she is taught, sanctified and guided until Christ returns by the Apostles through their successors who are the bishops in communion with the successor of Peter [emphasis added].
>
> Apostolic succession is the transmission by means of the sacrament of Holy Orders of the mission and power of the Apostles to their successors, the bishops. Thanks to this transmission the Church remains in communion of faith and life with her origin, which through the centuries she carries on her apostolate for the spread of the Kingdom of Christ on earth.[14]

---

[14] *Compendium of the Catechism of the Catholic Church* (Washington, D.C.: USCCB, 2013), 50.

The Catholic Church is apostolic in that it can *demonstrate* an unbroken line of succession traceable directly back to the Apostle Peter, and therefore, to Jesus Christ.

Chapter 5

The Unbroken Line of Apostolic Succession

Let no man do anything connected with the Church without the bishop.
(Bishop Ignatius of Antioch, AD 110)

✞ What I **discovered** ...

Jesus established a living Church, with divine authority, prior to the existence of a written Bible. He instituted leadership in a *visible* and hierarchal way so that His ministry would continue through the Holy Spirit. The Catholic Church, through an unbroken line of successors of Apostle Peter, demonstrates that it is founded upon the apostles and, therefore, Christ.

~ 🕮 ~

Jesus Establishes His Church

> And I tell you that you are **Peter**, and **upon this rock** I will **build my Church** and the gates of hell will **never** overcome it (Matthew 16:18).

Three striking facts are evident in this verse from Matthew's Gospel. First, Jesus established one *visible* Church on earth. Second, Jesus said He would build His Church *upon the rock* of Peter. Third, Jesus promised that the gates of hell will *never* prevail against the

Church He established, not then, not now. This promise is powerful, given that it *guarantees* the Church will exist from the time of Christ until He returns again. The Church, according to Jesus, will never dive into total apostasy such that Satan overcomes it. The establishment of Protestant churches, which departed from the apostolic Church over 1,500 years *later,* seems inconsistent with our Lord's promise of one perpetual Church.

As an extreme example of falling into the "apostasy theory" trap, consider Mormonism, which teaches there was a total apostasy after the last apostle died. Mormonism teaches that truth was taken from the earth until Joseph Smith "restored" it. In this example, Satan successfully overcame Jesus and His Church, a theory in conflict with our Lord's promise in Matthew 16:18!

Peter Receives *Unique* Authority

> I will give **you** the **keys** to the **kingdom of heaven**… (Matthew 16:19).

Notice how Jesus gives Peter the *keys* to the kingdom of heaven! Keys represent divinely appointed authority to preserve, teach, interpret, and lead. Peter is entrusted with *divine authority* to make decisions of faith that are binding on the Christian Church. This authority is unique and given to Peter alone.

In Isaiah 22:15-25, the Lord's servant Eliakim replaces Shebna as master of the palace. Eliakim will: 1) be given **the key** of the House of David, 2) be a **father** to the inhabitants of Jerusalem, and 3) have **authority** conferred upon him. The parallels, between this passage in Isaiah and our Lord giving Peter the keys, are profound. The keeper of the key moved with the *authority* of the king, a stunning picture of the authority given to Peter as he led with the *authority* of King Jesus! As Eliakim was the *father* of a people, so too is Peter the *father* of Christian people. Significantly, Pope means "papa" or "father."

Isaiah further writes, "what he opens, no one will shut, what he shuts, no one will open." The keys, then, are clear symbols of authority. The Protestant New Living Translation Study Bible comments, "The key to the House of David represents a high position of honor in the royal court (see also Rev 3:7). **When he opens doors...when he closes doors**: The officer with the **highest position** has sole authority in giving access to the king (cp. Matt 16:19)."[15] Peter, singularly given the key to the kingdom of heaven, is therefore entrusted with authority on earth to lead the Church.

Apostolic Authority to Bind and Loose

> ...whatever you **bind** on earth shall be **bound** in heaven and whatever you **loose** on earth shall be **loosed** in heaven (Matthew 16:19).

Peter is given the authority, by Christ, to *bind and loose* on earth with a corresponding action of binding and loosing that occurs in *heaven*! Here we find a direct reference to the divine authority to make authoritative

[15] *NLT Study Bible*, 2nd Edition (Carol Stream, IL: Tyndale House Publishers, 2008), 1140.

decisions on teaching. The power to "bind and loose on earth" was bestowed upon Peter and all the other apostles and their successors, the bishops (Matthew 18:18). We see that Peter has *both* the keys and binding and loosing authority, while the other apostles are given binding and loosing authority *only*.

Peter's Apostolic Primacy

Biblical evidence for Peter's primacy among the apostles is apparent throughout the Gospels and the Acts of the Apostles. Here are a few examples I found supportive of his primacy:

- **Peter** is named first, an implication of his primacy, in the list of apostles in the New Testament (Matthew 10:2-4, Mark 3:16-19, Luke 6:14-16, Acts of the Apostles 1:13).
- **Peter** received special revelation by God the Father (Matthew 16:15-17).
- **Peter** was singled out by name from an angel, distinguishing him from the other disciples at the tomb! (Mark 16:6-7).
- **Peter** is often specifically acknowledged, even when other apostles are present. The implication of authority is noticeable; for example, *Peter* and the other disciples, *Peter* and his companions, and the disciples and *Peter* (Mark 1:36, Luke 9:32).
- **Peter** proposed and presided over the election of Matthias to replace Judas Iscariot. The role of the apostles, particularly Peter, is evident in the apostolic replacement process (Acts of the Apostles 1:15-26).
- **Peter** was the first to preach the Good News on Pentecost (Acts of the Apostles 2:14-36).

- **Peter** was the first to lead a large baptism; the people accepted Peter's message and about 3,000 were saved! (Acts of the Apostles 2:37-41).
- **Peter** is specifically prayed over by Jesus, that his faith will not fail (Luke 22:31-32). Jesus charges Peter to build up and strengthen his brothers in the faith.
- **Peter** performs the first miracle of the apostles by healing a crippled beggar (Acts of the Apostles 3:1-10).
- **Peter** stands up and leads the debate at the First Council of Jerusalem (Acts of the Apostles 15:6-7).
- **Peter** reached the empty tomb after John. *However,* John stops and waits for Peter *before* entering! (John 20:1-10).
- **Peter** is the spokesman in most important events (e.g., John 6:67-69).
- **Peter**, James, and John were present with Jesus at the Transfiguration. Of the disciples, *only* Peter spoke (Matthew 17:1-8, Mark 9:2-8, Luke 9:28-36).
- **Peter** was specifically sought out by Cornelius at the direction of an angel (Acts 10:1-6).
- **Peter** was the first person after Christ to raise the dead (Acts 9:40).
- **Peter's** name is changed from Simon to Cephas (John 1:42):
  - Steve Ray highlights the importance of the name Cephas: "Cephas is the Greek transliteration of the Aramaic *Kepha*, which means 'rock.' Jesus tells Peter, 'You are Rock, and on this rock I

will build my church.'"[16] Jesus established His Church upon the rock of Peter!

– A name change signifies a special mission, a divine call to leadership. For example, recall Abram was renamed to Abraham as he was to be the "father" of many nations (Genesis 17:5).

– The physical location where Jesus calls Peter the rock is illuminating. The Bible says this happened when "Jesus came into the district of Caesarea Philippi" (Matthew 16:13). It is at this location that there stands a "gigantic wall of rock, a wall about 200 feet high and 500 feet long."[17] To the disciples, and all other listeners, the physical location removed any doubt that Peter is indeed the rock! "Jesus often chose a physical setting for making significant statements in his ministry, as evidenced by the Sermon on the Mount, Jacob's Well in Samaria, Mt. Horeb for the Transfiguration, and Jerusalem."[18]

---

[16] Stephen K. Ray, *St. John's Gospel: A Bible Study Guide and Commentary* (San Francisco, CA: Ignatius Press, 2002), 66.

[17] Catholic Answers, *Church & Papacy – Peter and the Papacy* (El Cajon, CA, 2004), pamphlet.

[18] Scott Butler, et al, *Jesus, Peter & the Keys,* (Santa Barbara, CA: Queenship Publishing, 1996), 13.

The Apostle Peter

Jesus builds His Church upon Peter.
Peter *singularly* receives the *keys* to the kingdom of heaven.
All apostles receive the authority to bind and loose, but Peter receives *both* the keys and binding and loosing authority.
Peter's primacy is proven in Scripture, apostolic Tradition, history, and theological logic.

Peter *is* the rock upon which Christ built His Church. The enormous amount of evidence in Scripture firmly establishes the primacy and authority of Peter among the other disciples.

Unbroken Line of Apostolic Succession

> Consequently, you are no longer foreigners and strangers, but fellow citizens with God's people and also members of his household, **built on the foundation of the apostles** and prophets, with Christ Jesus Himself as the chief cornerstone. In Him the whole building is joined together and rises to become a holy temple in the Lord (Ephesians 2:19-21).

The unbroken line of successors, linking directly back to the Apostle Peter, firmly establishes the apostolic origin and foundation of the Catholic Church. The

Biblical case for the succession of the apostles, from Peter to the current pope, is well anchored in history![19]

1) Peter	**AD 33 - 67**
2) Linus	67 - 76
3) Anacletus	76 - 88
4) Clement I	88 - 97
5) Evaristus	97 - 105
6) Alexander I	105 - 115
7) Sixtus I	115 - 125
8) Telesphorus	125 - 136
9) Hyginus	136 - 140
10) Pius I	140 - 155
11) Anicetus	155 - 166
12) Soter	166 - 175
13) Eleutherius	175 - 189
14) Victor I	189 - 199
15) Zephyrinus	199 - 217
16) Callistus	217 - 222
17) Urban I	222 - 230
18) Pontian	230 - 235
19) Anterus	235 - 236
20) Fabian	236 - 250
21) Cornelius	251 - 253

[19] Fr. Mario P. Romero, *Unabridged Christianity* (Goleta, CA: Queenship Publishing, 1999), 32-41. See also: Scott Butler, et al, *Jesus, Peter & the Keys*, (Santa Barbara, CA: Queenship Publishing, 1996), 375. The same list can be found at any public or university library. The historical list of popes can also be found by a simple Google search.

22) Lucius I	253 - 254
23) Stephen I	254 - 257
24) Sixtus I1	257 - 258
25) Dionysius	256 - 268
26) Felix I	269 - 274
27) Eutychian	275 - 283
28) Caius	283 - 296
29) Marcellinus	296 - 304
30) Marcellus I	308 - 309
31) Eusebius	309
32) Miltiades	311 - 314
33) Sil Vester I	314 - 335
34) Mark	336
35) Julius I	337 - 352
36) Liberius	352 - 366
37) Damasus I	366 - 384
38) Siricius	384 - 399
39) Anastasius I	399 - 401
40) Innocent I	401 - 417
41) Zosimus	417 - 418
42) Boniface I	418 - 422
43) Celestine I	422 - 432
44) Sixtus III	432 - 440
45) Leo I	440 - 461
46) Hilarus	461 - 468
47) Simplicius	468 - 483
48) Felix III	483 - 492
49) Gelasius I	492 - 496

50) Anastasius II	496 - 498
51) Symmachus	498 - 514
52) Hormisdas	514 - 523
53) John I	523 - 526
54) Felix IV	526 - 530
55) Boniface II	530 - 532
56) John II	533 - 535
57) Agapitus I	535 - 536
58) Silverius	536 - 537
59) Vigilius	537 - 555
60) Pelagius I	556 - 561
61) John III	561 - 574
62) Benedict I	575 - 579
63) Pelagius II	579 - 590
64) Gregory I	590 - 604
65) Sabinian	604 - 606
66) Boniface III	607
67) Boniface IV	608 - 615
68) Adeodatus	615 - 618
69) Boniface V	619 - 625
70) Honorius I	625 - 638
71) Severinus	640
72) John IV	640 - 642
73) Theodore I	642 - 649
74) Martin I	649 - 655
75) Eugene I	654 - 657
76) Vitalian	657 - 672
77) Adeodatus II	672 - 676

78) Donus	676 - 678
79) Agatho	678 - 681
80) Leo II	682 - 683
81) Benedict II	684 - 685
82) John V	685 - 686
83) Conon	686 - 687
84) Sergius I	687 - 701
85) John VI	701 - 705
86) John VII	705 - 707
87) Sissinius	708
88) Constantine	708 - 715
89) Gregory II	715 - 731
90) Gregory III	731 - 741
91) Zacharias	741 - 752
92) Stephen II	752 - 757
93) Paul I	757 - 767
94) Stephen III	768 - 772
95) Hadrian I	772 - 795
96) Leo III	795 - 816
97) Stephen IV	816 - 817
98) Paschal I	817 - 824
99) Eugene II	824 - 827
100) Valentine	827
101) Gregory IV	827 - 844
102) Sergius II	844 - 847
103) Leo IV	847 - 855
104) Benedict III	855 - 858
105) Nicholas	858 - 867

106) Hadrian II	867 - 872
107) John VIII	872 - 882
108) Marinus I	882 - 884
109) Hadrian III	884 - 885
110) Stephen V	885 - 891
111) Formosus	891 - 896
112) Boniface VI	896
113) Stephen VI	896 - 897
114) Romanus	897
115) Theodore II	897
116) John IX	898 - 900
117) Benedict IV	900 - 903
118) Leo V	903
119) Sergius III	904 - 911
120) Anastasius III	911 - 913
121) Lando	913 - 914
122) John X	914 - 928
123) Leo VI	928
124) Stephen VII	928 - 931
125) John XI	931 - 935
126) Leo VII	936 - 939
127) Stephen VIII	939 - 942
128) Marinus II	942 - 946
129) Agapitus II	946 - 955
130) John XII	955 - 964
131) Leo VIII	963 - 965
132) Benedict V	964 - 966
133) John XIII	965 - 972

134) Benedict VI	973 - 974
135) Benedict VII	974 - 983
136) John XIV	983 - 984
137) John XV	985 - 996
138) Gregory V	996 - 999
139) Silvester II	999 - 1003
140) John XVII	1003
141) John XVIII	1004 - 1009
142) Sergius IV	1009 - 1012
143) Benedict VIII	1012 - 1024
144) John XIX	1024 - 1032
145) Benedict IX	1032 - 1044
146) Silvester III	1045
147) Benedict IX	1045
148) Gregory VI	1045 - 1046
149) Clement II	1046 - 1047
150) Benedict IX	1047 - 1048
151) Damasus II	1048
152) Leo IX	1049 - 1054
153) Victor II	1055 - 1057
154) Stephen IX	1057 - 1058
155) Nicholas II	1059 - 1061
156) Alexander II	1061 - 1073
157) Gregory VII	1073 - 1085
158) Bl. Victor III	1086 - 1087
159) Bl. Urban II	1088 - 1099
160) Paschal II	1099 - 1118
161) Gelasius II	1118 - 1119

162) Callistus II	1119 - 1124
163) Honorius II	1124 - 1130
164) Innocent II	1130 - 1143
165) Celestine II	1143 - 1144
166) Lucius II	1144 - 1145
167) Bl. Eugene III	1145 - 1153
168) Anastasius IV	1153 - 1154
169) Hadrian IV	1154 - 1159
170) Alexander III	1159 - 1181
171) Lucius III	1181 - 1185
172) Urban III	1185 - 1187
173) Gregory VIII	1187
174) Clement III	1187 - 1191
175) Celestine III	1191 - 1198
176) Innocent III	1198 - 1216
177) Honorius III	1216 - 1227
178) Gregory IX	1227 - 1241
179) Celestine IV	1241
180) Innocent IV	1243 - 1254
181) Alexander IV	1254 - 1261
182) Urban IV	1261 - 1264
183) Clement IV	1265 - 1268
184) Bl. Gregory X	1272 - 1276
185) Bl. Innocent V	1276
186) Hadrian V	1276
187) John XXI	1276 - 1277
188) Nicholas III	1277 - 1280
189) Martin IV	1281 - 1285

190) Honorius IV	1285 - 1287
191) Nicholas IV	1288 - 1292
192) Celestine V	1294
193) Boniface VIII	1294 - 1303
194) Bl. Benedict XI	1303 - 1304
195) Clement V	1305 - 1314
196) John XXII	1316 - 1334
197) Benedict XII	1335 - 1342
198) Clement VI	1342 - 1352
199) Innocent VI	1352 - 1362
200) Bl. Urban V	1362 - 1370
201) Gregory XI	1371 - 1378
202) Urban VI	1378 - 1389
203) Boniface IX	1389 - 1404
204) Innocent VII	1404 - 1406
205) Gregory XII	1406 - 1415
206) Martin V	1417 - 1431
207) Eugene IV	1431 - 1447
208) Nicholas V	1447 - 1455
209) Callistus III	1455 - 1458
210) Pius II	1458 - 1464
211) Paul II	1464 - 1471
212) Sixtus IV	1471 - 1484
213) Innocent VIII	1484 - 1492
214) Alexander VI	1492 - 1503
215) Pius III	1503
216) Julius II	1503 - 1513
217) Leo X	1513 - 1521

218) Hadrian VI	1522 - 1523
219) Clement VII	1523 - 1534
220) Paul III	1534 - 1549
221) Jules III	1550 - 1555
222) Marcellus II	1555
223) Paul IV	1555 - 1559
224) Pius IV	1560 - 1565
225) Pius V	1566 - 1572
226) Gregory XIII	1572 - 1585
227) Sixtus V	1585 - 1590
228) Urban VII	1590
229) Gregory XIV	1590 - 1591
230) Innocent IX	1591
231) Clement VIII	1592 - 1605
232) Leo XI	1605
233) Paul V	1605 - 1621
234) Gregory XV	1621 - 1623
235) Urban VIII	1623 - 1644
236) Innocent X	1644 - 1655
237) Alexander VII	1655 - 1667
238) Clement IX	1667 - 1669
239) Clement X	1669 - 1676
240) Bl. Innocent XI	1676 - 1689
241) Alexander VIII	1689 - 1691
242) Innocent XII	1691 - 1700
243) Clement XI	1700 - 1721
244) Innocent XIII	1721 - 1724
245) Benedict XIII	1724 - 1730

246) Clement XII	1730 - 1740
247) Benedict XIV	1740 - 1758
248) Clement XIII	1758 - 1769
249) Clement XIV	1769 - 1774
250) Pius VI	1775 - 1799
251) Pius VII	1800 - 1823
252) Leo XII	1823 - 1829
253) Pius VIII	1829 - 1830
254) Gregory XVI	1831 - 1846
255) Pius IX	1846 - 1878
256) Leo XIII	1878 - 1903
257) Pius X	1903 - 1914
258) Benedict XV	1914 - 1922
259) Pius XI	1922 - 1939
260) Pius XII	1939 - 1958
261) John XXIII	1959 - 1963
262) Paul VI	1963 - 1978
263) John Paul I	1978
264) John Paul II	1978 - 2005
265) Benedict XVI	2005 - 2013
266) Pope Francis	**2013 - current**

Traceability to Apostle Peter provides concrete evidence that the Catholic Church has full apostolic origin through a *visible* and *unbroken line* of succession.

Only the Catholic Church existed in the tenth century, in the fifth century and in the first century, faithfully teaching the doctrines given by Christ to the apostles, omitting nothing. The line of popes can be traced back, in unbroken succession, to Peter himself. This is unequaled by any institution in history.[20]

I Was Shocked!

Researching the early Church, I was completely overtaken when I discovered that the first Christians testified to apostolic succession linking directly back to Peter. For example, Bishop Irenaeus, writing in the second century, amazingly records the names of the successors of Peter for the first 100 years! Irenaeus studied under Polycarp, who in turn, was a disciple of the Apostle John! Irenaeus writes:

> The blessed apostles, then, having founded and built up the Church, committed into the hands of **Linus**, the office of the episcopate. Of this **Linus**, Paul makes mention in the Epistles to Timothy [2 Timothy 4:21]. To him succeeded **Anacletus**; after him, in the third place from the apostles, **Clement** was allotted the bishopric (Irenaeus AD 180-199).[21]

Protestant Churches Have Popes, Too!

As an evangelical, born-again Christian, I was skeptical of authority. However, through time and honest reflection, I came to acknowledge that Protestant

---

[20] *Pillar of Fire, Pillar of Truth* (San Diego, CA: Catholic Answers, 1997), 2.

[21] Irenaeus, *Against Heresies* (Beloved Publishing, 2015), 207.

churches have authorities too. A senior pastor, committee, or board usually determines what their particular denomination or ministry believe. The statement of faith is typically captured in church "bylaws" (leader title, pastoral offices, elders, voting structure, qualifications, faith statement, and so on). James L. Papandrea makes a similar observation:

> But even those congregational and non-denominational congregations and "mega-Churches" that might criticize the Catholic Church for having a pope must necessarily have their own highest authority when it comes to matters of doctrine and the interpretation of Scripture. In other words, they all have their own "pope" (usually their founding pastor) who speaks for the whole group and settles disputes. If they didn't have this, they would soon split over differences of opinion. Many of them do anyway. The pope speaks for the Church that is headquartered at Rome, but with the authority of 2,000 years of Tradition behind him.[22]

What Protestant church today can speak with 2,000 years of authority? Those that attack the authority of the Catholic Church are forced into declaring their own infallible authority, typically the pastor of their own church, denomination, or ministry. Jeff Cavins confirms a similar observation:

---

[22] James L. Papandrea, *Handed Down* (El Cajun, CA: Catholic Answers Press, 2015), 203.

So while anti-Catholics attack the teaching authority of Peter and his successors, they do so based on their *own* authority as the final judge of Scripture. In reality this means that they have set themselves up as pope![23]

What the Church Fathers and Early Christians Believed About Peter, Authority, and Apostolic Succession.

Clement of Rome, *Letter to the Corinthians* (AD 80):

> Similarly, our Apostles knew, through our Lord Jesus Christ, that there would be dissensions over the title of bishop. In their full foreknowledge of this, therefore, they proceeded to appoint the ministers I spoke of, and they went on to add an instruction that if these should fall asleep, other accredited persons should **succeed them in their office.**[24]

Ignatius of Antioch, *Letter to the Ephesians* (AD 110):

> For Jesus Christ, our inseparable life, is the will of the Father, just as the **bishops**, who have been **appointed** throughout the world, are the will of Jesus Christ. It is fitting, therefore, that you should live in

[23] Cavins, 58.

[24] *Early Christian Writings: The Apostolic Fathers* (Penguin Classics, 1987), 41.

> harmony with the will of the **bishop**—as indeed, you do. Let us be careful, then, if we would be submissive to God, **not to oppose the bishop.**[25]

Ignatius of Antioch, *Letter to the Trallians* (AD 110):

> Indeed, **when you submit to the bishop** as you would to Jesus Christ, it is clear to me that you are living not in the manner of men but as Jesus Christ, who died for us, that through faith in His death you might escape dying. It is necessary, therefore—and such is your practice—**that you do nothing without the bishop**, and that you be subject also to the presbytery, as to the Apostles of Jesus Christ our hope, in whom we shall be found, if we live in him.[26]

Ignatius of Antioch, *Letter to the Smyrnaeans* (AD 110):

> You must all **follow the bishop** as Jesus Christ follows the Father, and the presbytery as you would the **apostles**. Reverence the **deacons** as you would the command of God. **Let no one do anything of concern to the Church without the bishop**. Let that be considered a valid Eucharist which is celebrated by the **bishop**, or by one whom he appoints. **Wherever the bishop appears, let the people be there; just as**

[25] William A. Jurgens, *The Faith of the Early Fathers*, Vol. 1 (Collegeville, MN: The Liturgical Press, 1970), 17-18.

[26] Ibid., 20.

> **wherever Jesus Christ is, there is the Catholic Church**.[27]

Irenaeus of Lyons, *Against Heresies* (AD 180-199):

> It is within the power of all, therefore, in every **Church**, who may wish to see the truth, to contemplate clearly the **tradition of the apostles** manifested throughout the whole world; and we are in a position to reckon up those who were **by the apostles** instituted **bishops** in the **Churches**, and to demonstrate the **succession** of these men **to our own times**; those who neither taught nor knew of anything like what these heretics rave about.[28]
>
> Since, however, it would be very tedious, in such a volume as this, to reckon up the **successions** of all the **Churches**, we do put to confusion all those who, in whatever manner, whether by an evil self-pleasing, by vainglory, or by blindness and perverse opinion, assemble in unauthorized meetings; [we do this, I say,] by indicating that **tradition derived from the apostles,** of the very great, the very ancient, and **universally known Church founded and organized at Rome** by the two most glorious apostles, **Peter and Paul**; as also by pointing out the faith preached to men,

---

[27] Ibid., 25.

[28] Irenaeus, *Against Heresies* (Beloved Publishing, 2015), 206-207.

which comes down to our time by means of the **successions of the bishops**. For it is a matter of necessity that **every Church should agree with this Church,** on account of its **preeminent authority**, that is, the faithful everywhere, inasmuch as the apostolical tradition has been preserved continuously by those faithful men who exist everywhere.[29]

But **Polycarp** also was not only **instructed by apostles**, and conversed with many who had seen Christ, but was also, by **apostles** in Asia, **appointed bishop of the Church** in Smyrna, whom I also saw in my early youth, for he tarried on earth a very long time, and, when a very old man, gloriously and most nobly suffering martyrdom, departed this life, having always taught the things which he had **learned from the apostles**, and which **the Church has handed down**, and which alone are true. To these things all the Asiatic Churches testify, as do also those men who have **succeeded** Polycarp down to the present time…[30]

Wherefore it is incumbent to **obey** the **presbyters** who are in the **Church**—those who, as I have shown, possess the **succession from the apostles**; those who, together with the **succession** of the episcopate, have

[29] Ibid., 207.
[30] Ibid., 208.

> received the certain gift of truth, according to the good pleasure of the Father. But it is also incumbent to hold in suspicion others **who depart** from the primitive **succession**, and assemble themselves together in any place whatsoever, looking upon them either as heretics of perverse minds, or as schismatics puffed up and self-pleasing, or again as hypocrites, acting thus for the sake of lucre and vainglory. For all these have fallen from the truth. And the heretics, indeed, who bring strange fire to the altar of God— namely, strange doctrines…[31]

> **True knowledge** is [that which consists in] the **doctrine of the apostles**, and the ancient constitution of the **Church** throughout all the world, and the distinctive manifestation of the body of Christ according to the **successions of the bishops**, by which they have **handed down that Church** which exists in every place, and has come even unto us, being guarded and preserved without any forging of Scriptures, by a very complete system of doctrine…[32]

Ambrose, Bishop of Milan (AD 338-397):

> Moreover, that you may know that it is after His Manhood that He entreats, and in virtue of His Godhead that He commands,

[31] Ibid., 367-368.
[32] Ibid., 389-390.

> it is written for you in the Gospel that He said to **Peter**: "I have prayed for you, that your faith fail not." Luke 22:32. **To the same Apostle**, again, when on a former occasion he said, "You are the Christ, the Son of the living God," He made answer: "**You are Peter**, and **upon this Rock will I build My Church**, and **I will give you the keys of the kingdom of heaven**." Matthew 16:18. Could He not, then, strengthen the faith of the man to whom, acting on His own authority, He gave the kingdom, **whom He called the Rock**, thereby **declaring him to be the foundation of the Church?**[33]

Cyril of Jerusalem (AD 350):

> The Lord is loving toward men, swift to pardon, but slow to punish. Let no man, then, despair of his own salvation. **Peter, the first and foremost of the Apostles**, denied the Lord three times before a little servant girl, but he repented and wept bitterly. Weeping is demonstrative of repentance from the depth of the heart, which is why he not only received the forgiveness of his denial, but also kept his **Apostolic dignity without forfeit.**[34]

---

[33] *Exposition of the Christian Faith*, Book IV, Chapter 5, Paragraph 57.

[34] William A. Jurgens, *The Faith of the Early Fathers*, Vol. 1 (Collegeville, MN: The Liturgical Press, 1970), 348.

> In the power of the same Holy Spirit, **Peter,** both **the chief of the Apostles** and **the keeper of the keys of the kingdom of heaven**, in the name of Christ healed Aeneas the paralytic at Lydda, which is now called Diospolis; and at Joppa he raised the beneficent Tabitha from the dead.[35]

Jerome (AD 347 – 420):

> Wherever there is a **bishop**, whether it be at Rome or at Engubium, whether it be at Constantinople or at Rhegium, whether it be at Alexandria or at Zoan, his dignity is one and his priesthood is one. Neither the command of wealth nor the lowliness of poverty makes him more a bishop or less a bishop. **All alike are successors of the apostles.**[36]

Jerome, Letter to Pope Damasus (AD 377):

> I think it my duty to **consult the chair of Peter**, and to turn to a church whose faith has been praised by Paul… My words are spoken to the **successor** of the fisherman, to the disciple of the cross. As I follow no leader save Christ, so I communicate with none but your blessedness, that is with **the chair of Peter**. For this, I know, is **the rock** on which the **church is built**![37]

---

[35] Ibid., 358.

[36] Philip Schaff, *Nicene and Post-Nicene Fathers*, Series II, Vol. 6 (Letter CXLVI to Evangelus), 680.

[37] Ibid.

I was jubilant upon discovering the Biblical and historical evidence that firmly demonstrates Jesus established *one* visible Church. His Church continues today through an unbroken line of apostolic succession! My Baptist tradition, and in fact *all* Protestant traditions, can only trace their lineage back a few hundred years to the man, Martin Luther. It was extremely humbling to discover the enormous amount of evidence proving, without dispute, the Church Fathers and all early Christians unanimously believed, taught, and followed apostolic succession.

Chapter 6

Our Bread of Life

I hunger for the bread of God, the flesh of Jesus Christ...;
I long to drink of his blood, the gift of unending love.
(Bishop Ignatius of Antioch, AD 110)

✝ What I **discovered** ...

The Eucharist is not *symbolic* of Christ, but literally *is* Christ. In this mystery of faith, celebrated at every Catholic Mass for 2,000 years, bread and wine are transubstantiated into the body and blood of Jesus through the power of the Holy Spirit. This was believed by all Christians, in all places, at all times until the Protestant Reformation! The resurrected Jesus is truly present in this powerful and efficacious Sacrament referred to as the "Real Presence." For apostolic Christians, Holy Communion is the absolute center of worship!

The Last Supper: "This *is* my body...This *is* my blood"

Jesus instituted the Holy Eucharist at the Last Supper. Matthew, Mark, and Luke each provide an account:

> While they were eating, Jesus took bread, and when he had given thanks, he broke it and gave it to his disciples, saying, "Take

> and eat; **this *is* my body**." Then he took a cup, and when he had given thanks, he gave it to them, saying, "Drink from it, all of you. **This *is* my blood** of the covenant, which is poured out for many for the forgiveness of sins" (Matthew 26:26-28).
>
> While they were eating he took bread, said the blessing, broke it, and gave it to them, and said, "Take it; **this *is* my body**." Then he took a cup, gave thanks, and gave it to them, and they all drank from it. He said to them, "**This *is* my blood** of the covenant, which will be shed for many" (Mark 14:22-24).
>
> Then he took the bread, said the blessing, broke it, and gave it to them, saying, "**This *is* my body**, which will be given for you; do this in memory of me." And likewise the cup after they had eaten, saying, "This cup is the new covenant **in *my* blood**, which will be shed for you" (Luke 22:19-20).

Jesus declares "this *is* my body" and "this *is* my blood." There is no indication that Jesus was speaking metaphorically or symbolically, as affirmed in the Greek. A straightforward reading of what Jesus *actually* said in the three Synoptic Gospel's immediately leads to a literal understanding of the body and blood of Jesus being offered in the Holy Eucharist.

"Their eyes were opened"

> And it happened that, while he was with them at the table, he took bread, said the blessing, broke it, and gave it to them. With that **their eyes were opened** and they recognized him, but he vanished from their sight… Then the two recounted what had taken place on the way and **how he was made known to them in the breaking of the bread** (Luke 24:30-35).

We partake in the resurrected body and blood of Jesus through faith. In the mystical Eucharist, our eyes are opened to see Jesus and His miracles in a personal way.

Preparing for the Mystery of Faith

In the sixth chapter of the Gospel of John, we read about multiple miracles: The miracle of the multiplication of the loaves (John 6:1-15), Jesus walking on water (John 6:16-21), and the Bread of Life discourse (John 6:22-59). These miracles are related, and one prepares the reader for the next. As in the case of feeding the multitudes, so is the case of Christ feeding us His body and blood in the Lord's Supper. Jesus multiplies the loaves and fish, a miracle which *foreshadows* His ability to multiply His presence in the Eucharist.[38] We are His multitudes, the mystical body of Christ. Jesus was preparing the people (and us) to receive the miracle of His Real Presence. Feeding the multitudes was not

[38] Oscar Lukefahr, *"We Believe… ": A Survey of the Catholic Faith* (Liguori, MO: Liguori Publications, 1990), 104.

symbolic. Jesus walking on water was not symbolic. What happens next, the Eucharist, is equally not symbolic. The people approach Jesus and ask what they must do in order to be doing the works of God. Jesus replies that belief is required:

> So they said to him, "What can we do to accomplish the works of God?" Jesus answered and said to them, "This is the work of God that you **believe** in the one he sent" (John 6:28-29).

The essential aspect of the Gospel is to *believe* in Jesus Christ as Lord and Savior. We are also to *believe* every word that comes from the mouth of God, including the Eucharist! It is *by faith* we come to see and understand spiritual things of God. We are united with Christ through faith in this beautiful Sacrament.

The Disciples Interpret Jesus *Literally*

Continuing John's Gospel and the Bread of Life discourse, observe that God the Father draws people to believe. Jesus reiterates that faith in Christ is required for salvation and to receive His miracles:

> No one can come to me **unless the Father** who sent me **draws him**, and I will raise him on the last day… Amen, amen, I say to you, whoever **believes** has eternal life. I am the **bread of life** (John 6:44, 47-48).

Jesus declares that the bread is His *flesh*:

> I am the living bread that came down from heaven; whoever eats this bread will live

> forever; and the bread that I will give **is my flesh** for the life of the world (John 6:51).

Hearing this, the disciples become unsettled and begin arguing:

> The Jews **quarreled** among themselves, saying, "How can this man give us **his flesh** to eat?" (John 6:52).

The disciples clearly understand Jesus to be speaking *literally*! Jesus does not correct them, but He does confirm the truth by a double "amen, amen" that in fact it is His flesh and blood that He is speaking about!

> Jesus said to them, "**Amen, amen,** I say to you, unless you **eat the flesh** of the Son of Man and **drink his blood**, you do not have life within you. Whoever **eats my flesh** and **drinks my blood** has eternal life, and I will raise him on the last day. For **my flesh is true food, and my blood is true drink**. Whoever **eats my flesh** and **drinks my blood** remains in me and I in him" (John 6:53-56).

In John 6:51, the Greek word *phago* is used which means "to eat or consume." When the Jews began quarrelling over the correct interpretation, Jesus replied with a much stronger verb, *trogo*, which means to "chew, gnaw, or crunch" (John 6:54, 56-58). Jesus reinforces a literal, *not* symbolic, understanding of "eating" His flesh by this dramatic shift in the Greek, thereby removing any doubt about the correct interpretation.

What happens next is equally supportive. Scripture, sadly, says that some disciples became startled and stopped following Jesus. Why? They understood Christ to be speaking literally of His body and blood, which caused them great fear.

> These things he said while teaching in the synagogue in Capernaum. Then many of his disciples who were listening said, "**This saying is hard; who can accept it?**" Since Jesus knew that his disciples were murmuring about this, he said to them, "Does this **shock you**? What if you were to see the Son of Man ascending to where he was before? It is the **spirit that gives life**, while the **flesh is of no avail**. The words I have spoken to you **are spirit** and life. But there are some of you who **do not believe**." Jesus knew from the beginning the ones who would not believe and the one who would betray him. And he said, "For this reason I have told you that no one can come to me unless it is granted him by my Father." As a result of this, **many of his disciples returned to their former way of life and no longer accompanied him** (John 6:59-66).

Unbelief caused many disciples to stop following Jesus. Like the virgin birth of Christ and His resurrection, by faith we receive the Holy Eucharist.

Right here in Scripture, we see the first recorded "apostasy" in New Testament history! Did you catch that my friend? They left Jesus over His teaching on the Eucharist! At the root is their *unbelief*. Notice how Jesus said that even if they were to see Him ascending, they would not have *believed* it. In the flesh, we cannot understand how Jesus literally gives us His real body and blood. By the Spirit we come to understand the mystical works of Christ.

> The person without the Spirit does not accept the things that come from the Spirit of God but considers them foolishness, and **cannot understand** them because they are discerned only through the Spirit (1 Corinthians 2:14).

If we do not open our hearts by faith, we will not experience the mystical works of Christ in our life! They denied the Real Presence of Jesus in the Eucharist, just as many still do today.

Not a Single Clarification!

There is a trend in the Gospel of John worth noting and applicable directly to our discussion. John frequently provides clarifications when misunderstandings occur and guides the reader to see the correct interpretation. When Jesus spoke symbolically, and the Jews understood Him literally, John adds clarification. For example, when Jesus spoke of the temple being His body (e.g., the Jews misunderstood) John appends clarification. Likewise, when Jesus speaks of living water, they misunderstand but John again offers consistent clarification.

> Jesus answered them, "Destroy this temple, and in three days I will raise it up." The

> Jews then said, "It has taken forty-six years to build this temple, and will you raise it up in three days?" **But he was speaking** about the temple of his body (John 2:19-21).
>
> On the last and greatest day of the festival, Jesus stood and said in a loud voice, "Let anyone who is thirsty come to me and drink. Whoever believes in me, as Scripture has said, rivers of living water will flow from within them." **By this he meant** the Spirit, whom those who believed in him were later to receive. Up to that time the Spirit had not been given, since Jesus had not yet been glorified (John 7:37-39).
>
> Then they said to him, "Who are you?" And Jesus said to them, "Just as I have been saying to you from the beginning. I have many things to say and to judge concerning you, but he who sent me is true; and I speak to the world those things which I heard from him." **They did not understand that** he spoke to them of the Father (John 8:25-27).

John took great care to point out misunderstandings in his Gospel. In the case of the body and blood of Jesus, neither Jesus nor John offers any clarification!

Discerning the Lord's Body in the Eucharist

Scripture has words of caution for those who refuse to discern the Lord's body in the Eucharist. The Apostle Paul says:

> He who eats and drinks in an unworthy manner eats and drinks judgment to himself, **not discerning the Lord's body** (1 Corinthians 11:29).

If the Lord's Supper, the Eucharist, were merely a *symbol* it seems strange to see how such judgment could occur.

Consuming Christ!

Jesus, the "Lamb of God, who takes away the sin of the world" (John 1:29) ushers in a New Passover and a New Covenant with the people of God. Luke explains that "this cup is the **new covenant** in my blood" (Luke 22:20). Joseph Cardinal Ratzinger offers this explanation:

> The symbolic value of the Twelve is consequently of decisive significance: twelve is the number of Jacob's sons, the number of the twelve tribes of Israel. In constituting the circle of Twelve, Jesus presents himself as the patriarch of a new Israel and institutes these twelve men as its origin and foundation. There could be no clearer way of expressing the beginning of a new people, which is now no longer formed by physical descent but by "being with Jesus..."[39]

---

[39] Joseph Cardinal Ratzinger, *Called to Communion: Understanding the Church Today* (San Francisco, CA: Ignatius Press, 1996), 25.

As Ratzinger points out, God established a New Covenant which is characterized by being with Jesus. Ratzinger continues:

> On the night before his Passion, Jesus took another decisive step beyond this: he transformed the Passover of Israel into an entirely new worship, which logically meant a break with the temple community and thereby definitively established a people of the "New Covenant."[40]

We are in a New Covenant relationship with God that is not built using a temple or walls, but by Someone much greater! Ratzinger finishes the thought:

> The sense of all this is clear: "Just as the **old Israel** once revered the temple as its **center** and the guarantee of **its unity**, and by its common celebration of the Passover enacted this unity in its own life, in like manner this **new meal** is now the bond **uniting a new people of God**. There is no longer any need for a center localized in an outward temple...**The Body of the Lord**, which **is the center of the Lord's Supper**, is the one new temple that joins Christians together into a much more **real unity** than a temple made of stone could ever do... It could be said that the people of the New Covenant takes its **origin as a people from the Body and Blood of Christ**; solely in terms of this **center does**

[40] Ibid., 26.

> **it have the status of a people.** We can call it 'people of God' only because it is through communion with Christ that man gains access to a relationship with God that he cannot establish by his own power."[41]

Evangelical Protestant churches place a pulpit at the center of the worship area. In stark contrast, the Catholic Church has always placed an altar at the center. Thus, for the apostolic Church, the supreme *focal point* of worship is the Eucharist! In this way, the apostolic Church is especially *Christ*-centric!

Protestantism is *pastor*-centric, while apostolic Christianity is *Eucharist*-centric. The center of the former is a *sermon*, while the center of the latter is the *Real Presence* of Christ!

The Eucharist is Real Communion

> The cup of blessing which we bless, is it not the communion of the *blood* of Christ? The bread which we break, is it not the communion of the *body* of Christ? (1 Corinthians 10:16).

The body and blood of Jesus is the *uniting center* for Christians. Can Christians have communion of the "blood of Christ" and "body of Christ" if the bread and wine are mere symbols?

---

[41] Ibid., 27-29.

New Manna for the New Exodus!

From the Old Testament to the New Testament, we move from symbol to reality. In the Old Testament, God miraculously fed His people manna during their journey to the Promised Land (Exodus 16). In the New Testament, Jesus equates Himself to the new manna, the Bread of Life (John 6:30-51). When reading the New Testament in light of the Old Testament, the Eucharistic implications are simply stunning!

The manna was real food, not symbolic. Jesus is a real Person, not symbolic. The Word became flesh and made His dwelling among us! (John 1:14). Because the Old Covenant is a foreshadowing of the New Covenant, the new manna must be superior and more perfect than the first manna. If the new manna is only a symbol, how can this be superior and more perfect than the old manna? Jesus is superior, and the new manna must also be superior!

> Now consider which is more excellent, the bread of angels [i.e., the manna] or the Flesh of Christ which is indeed the Body of life. That manna was from heaven; this is from above the heavens. The former was from heaven, the latter from the Lord of the heavens; the former was subject to corruption if it was preserved for a second day, the latter foreign to all corruption....[42]

In the Old Testament, God miraculously provided real manna from heaven to feed the Israelites as

---

[42] James T. O'Connor, *The Hidden Manna: A Theology of the Eucharist* (San Francisco, CA: Ignatius Press, 2005), 37.

they wondered through the wilderness to the Promised Land. In the New Testament, Christians are fed an even greater Manna, the Real Presence, during our exodus from the slavery of sin in this life until we reach our Promised Land—which is heaven!

Jewish Roots of the Eucharist

The Last Supper took place in the historical context of the Jewish Passover found in the Old Testament book of Exodus. The Israelites were enslaved in the land of Egypt under Pharaoh. In order to induce freedom for God's people, the Lord sent a plague that would kill all firstborn Egyptians, animals included. However, the Israelites were promised that they would be saved if they would perform a ritual described by God (Exodus 12:3-14). The Israelites were told to sacrifice a male lamb that was pure and spotless. None of the bones of this lamb were to be broken. The Israelites were then told to put the blood of the sacrificial lamb on their doorway and doorposts, so that, when the Lord "passed over" their homes, the destroyer would not harm them. They would be saved by the blood of the Paschal lamb.

The Paschal lamb described in the Old Testament is clearly a foreshadowing of Jesus in the New Testament. John announced, "Behold the Lamb of God who takes away the sin of the world" (John 1:29). The spotless, sacrificial Lamb, whose bones were never broken, is our resurrected hope and salvation. It is through the life, death, and resurrection of Jesus (our Passover Lamb) that we are saved. He replaces the lamb with Himself, the Divine Lamb!

The Jewish Passover offers profound insight into understanding the origins of the Holy Eucharist. Brant Pitre, in *Jesus and the Jewish Roots of the Eucharist,* captures a powerful moment at the Last Supper:

> But at his final Passover, on the night of the Last Supper, Jesus did something strange. During that meal, instead of speaking about the past exodus from Egypt, Jesus talked about his future suffering and death. On that night, instead of explaining the meaning of the flesh of the Passover lamb, Jesus identified the bread and wine of the supper as his own body and blood, and, commanded the disciples to eat and drink. Why?[43]

The ancient Jewish roots of the Passover shed light on the reason why a *literal* understanding of the Eucharist is both Biblical and historical. The five essential steps in the Jewish Passover meal are to:

1) Choose an unblemished male lamb.

2) Sacrifice the lamb.

3) Spread the blood of the lamb on the home as a "sign" of the sacrifice.

4) **Eat the flesh of the lamb** with unleavened bread [emphasis added].

5) Every year, keep the Passover as a "day of remembrance" of the exodus forever.[44]

---

[43] Brant Pitre, *Jesus and the Jewish Roots of the Eucharist* (Doubleday, 2011), 49.

[44] Ibid., 58.

In evangelical Protestant Christianity, the Lord's Supper is held in "remembrance" of His sacrifice for our sins. But this is only half of the meal! As Pitre points out, in the Jewish Passover, the meal was not *complete* until the lamb was *actually eaten* or *consumed.* Eating the flesh of the lamb was part of the meal. The implications of this historical fact, when related to the New Testament Passover Lamb, are simply staggering. Why? If eating the lamb in the Old Testament Passover were *symbolic*, it would lend evidence to a symbolic equivalent of the New Testament Last Supper. However, the Old Testament Jewish Passover required a *literal* lamb to be eaten, thus, when Jesus says, "this *is* my body" and "this *is* my blood," we understand Him to be speaking literally based on the Jewish roots of The Passover. A *symbol* can never make sense in this context. It is precisely for this reason that I believe Paul says that Christ is our Passover Lamb, therefore, "let us keep the feast" (1 Corinthians 5:8).

Figurative Gibberish

The language spoken by Christ does not allow for a figurative or symbolic meaning. To force a figurative understanding ends in an errant expression!

> In the Aramaic language of our Lord, to figuratively "eat the flesh" or "drink the blood" of someone meant to persecute, assault, and destroy him. This Hebrew expression is found in many Scripture passages... If Jesus is speaking only *figuratively* about eating His flesh and drinking His blood, as many non-Catholics

> claim, then what He really means is "*whoever persecutes, assaults, and destroys Me will have eternal life.*" This makes nonsense of the passage![45]

Protestant Reformation *founder* Martin Luther (AD 1483–1546) on the Real Presence of Jesus in the Eucharist

Along my faith journey, I always anticipated most of Martin Luther's beliefs would be anti-Catholic. However, what I discovered is considerably different! Before the Protestant Reformation, *hardly any* Christians believed in a symbolic or figurative Lord's Supper; to the contrary, *all* Christians believed in the Real Presence of Jesus in Communion! While not all reformers adhered to his teachings, Martin Luther personally believed in the Real Presence of Christ!

> Now here stands the Word of Christ: *Take, eat; this is My body; Drink ye all of it; this is the new testament in My blood*... But if the words remain with them, as they shall and must, then, in virtue of the same, **it is truly the body and blood of Christ.** For as the lips of Christ say and speak, so it is, as He can never lie or deceive.[46]

---

[45] Father Frank Chacon and Jim Burnham, *Beginning Apologetics 3* (Farmington, NM: San Juan Catholic Seminars, 2014), 13-14.

[46] Martin Luther, *The Essential Martin Luther*, A Christian Classic (Start Publishing, eBook, 2012).

> For my part, if I cannot fathom how the bread is the Body of Christ, yet **I will take my reason captive to the obedience of Christ** (1 Corinthians 10:5), and clinging simply to his words, **firmly believe not only that the Body of Christ is in the bread but that the bread is the Body of Christ**... What does it matter if philosophy cannot fathom this? The Holy Spirit is greater than Aristotle.[47]

Luther believed that Christ's body and blood are truly present in the Holy Eucharist. Further, Luther dogmatically proclaimed that every Church Father since the time of the apostles believed in the Real Presence, too!

> Who, but the devil, hath granted such a license of wrestling the words of the holy Scripture? Who ever read in the Scriptures, that my body is the same as the sign of my body? Or, that is the same as it signifies? What language in the world ever spoke so? It is only then the devil, that imposeth upon us by these fanatical men.... **Not one of the Fathers**, though so numerous, ever spoke as the Sacramentarians: **not one of them ever said, It is only bread and wine; or, the body and blood of Christ is not there present.** Surely it is not credible, not possible, since they often speak, and

[47] James T. O'Connor, *The Hidden Manna: A Theology of the Eucharist* (San Francisco, CA: Ignatius Press, 2005), 136.

> repeat their sentiments, that they should never (if they thought so) not so much as once, say, or let slip these words: It is bread only; or the body of Christ is not there, especially it being of great importance, that men should not be deceived. Certainly in so many Fathers, and in so many writings, the negative might at least be found in one of them, had they thought the body and blood of Christ were not really present; **but they are all of them unanimous**.[48]

The disciples, apostles, early Church Fathers, and the *founder* of the Protestant Reformation Martin Luther all believed in the Real Presence of Christ in the Eucharist. Unfortunately, Protestant Reformation leaders Ulrich Zwingli and John Calvin soon broke away from this 1,600 year apostolic teaching and began spreading their own individual ideas on the Holy Eucharist. Zwingli broke with Luther and believed that the Eucharist was only a symbol. Calvin disagreed and believed the Eucharist to be greater than a symbol, but less than the Real Presence of Christ. If you are in a Protestant tradition today, to which of these three Protestant Reformation founders should you turn to find truth? Sadly, modern Protestantism has departed, *not only* from 1,600 years of apostolic teaching, but *even their own founder's teachings!*

---

[48] Martin Luther, *Luther's Collected Works*, Wittenberg Edition, Vol. VII, 391.

What the Church Fathers and Early Christians Believed *About the Eucharist.*

The Didache, Greek for "The Teaching of the Twelve," one of the earliest Christian documents outside the Bible (AD 50-80), teaches:

> No one is to **eat or drink of your Eucharist** but those who have been baptized in the Name of the Lord; for the Lord's own saying applies here, "Give not **that which is holy** unto dogs."[49]

Ignatius of Antioch (AD 110):

> Earthly longings have been crucified; in me there is left no spark of desire for mundane things, but only a murmur of living water that whispers within me, "Come to the Father." There is no pleasure for me in any meats that perish, or in the delights of this life; I am fain for the bread of God, even the **flesh of Jesus Christ**, who is the seed of David; and for my drink **I crave the Blood of His** which is love imperishable.[50]

> **They abstain from the Eucharist** and from prayer **because they do not confess** that the Eucharist is the **Flesh** of our Savior Jesus Christ, **Flesh** which suffered for our sins and which the Father, in His goodness,

[49] *Early Christian Writings: The Apostolic Fathers* (Penguin Classics, 1987), 195.

[50] Ibid., 87.

> raised up again. They who deny the gift of God are perishing in their disputes.[51]

Justin Martyr (AD 100-165):

> We call this food *Eucharist*; and no one else is permitted to partake of it, except one who believes our teaching to be true and who has been washed in the washing which is for the remission of sins and for regeneration, and is thereby living as Christ has enjoined. **For not as common bread nor common drink do we receive these**; but since Jesus Christ our Savior was made incarnate by the word of God and had both flesh and blood for our salvation, so too, as we have been taught, the food which has been made into the Eucharist by the **Eucharist prayer** set down by Him, and by the **change** of which our blood and flesh is nourished, **is both the flesh and the blood of that incarnated Jesus.**[52]

Irenaeus of Lyons, *Against Heresies* (AD 180-199):

> But how can they be consistent with themselves, when they say that the bread over which thanks have been given **is the body of their Lord, and the cup His blood**, if they do not call Himself the Son of the Creator of the world, that is, His Word... Then, again, how can they say

[51] William A. Jurgens, *The Faith of the Early Fathers*, Vol. 1 (Collegeville, MN: The Liturgical Press, 1970), 25.

[52] Ibid., 55.

> that the flesh, which is nourished with the **body** of the Lord and with **His blood**, goes to corruption, and does not partake of life? Let them, therefore, either alter their opinion, or cease from offering the things just mentioned. **But our opinion** is in accordance with the **Eucharist**, and the **Eucharist** in turn **establishes our opinion**. For we offer to Him His own, announcing consistently the fellowship and union of the flesh and Spirit. **For as the bread**, which is produced from the earth, **when it receives the invocation of God, is no longer common bread, but the Eucharist, consisting of two realities, earthly and heavenly**; so also our bodies, when they receive the Eucharist, are no longer corruptible, having the hope of the resurrection to eternity.[53]

Cyprian, Bishop of Carthage (died AD 258):

> And who is more a priest of the Most High God, than our Lord Jesus Christ, who, when He offered sacrifice to God the Father, offered the very same which Melchisedech had offered, namely bread and wine**, which is in fact His Body and Blood!**[54]

Cyril of Jerusalem, *Catechetical Lectures* (AD 350):

> For just as the bread and the wine of the Eucharist **before the holy invocation** of

---

[53] Irenaeus, *Against Heresies* (Beloved Publishing, 2015), 345.
[54] Jurgens, 232.

> the adorable Trinity were simple bread and wine, **but the invocation** having been made, the bread **becomes the Body of Christ**, and the **wine the Blood of Christ**...[55]

Ambrose, Bishop of Milan (AD 338-397):

> You may perhaps say: "My bread is ordinary." But that bread is bread **before the words of the Sacraments**; where the consecration has entered in, the **bread becomes the flesh of Christ.** And let us add this: How can what is bread be the Body of Christ? **By the consecration.** The consecration takes place by certain words; but whose words? Those of the Lord Jesus. Like all the rest of the things said beforehand, **they are said by the priest**; praises are referred to God, prayer of petition is offered for the people, for kings, for other persons; but when the time comes for the confection of the venerable Sacrament, **then the priest uses not his own words but the words of Christ. Therefore it is the word of Christ that confects this Sacrament.**[56]

Augustine, Bishop of Hippo (AD 354-430):

> That Bread which you see on the altar, having been sanctified by the word of God, **is the Body of Christ.** That chalice, or

---

[55] Ibid., 359.

[56] William A. Jurgens, *The Faith of the Early Fathers*, Vol. 2 (Collegeville, MN: The Liturgical Press, 1970), 176.

> rather, what is in that chalice, having been sanctified by the word of God, **is the Blood of Christ.**[57]

> What you see is the bread and the chalice; that is what your **own eyes report to you**. But what your **faith** obliges you to accept is that **the bread is the Body of Christ** and the **chalice is the Blood of Christ.**[58]

John of Damascene (AD 645-749):

> The Bread and the Wine are **not a type** of the Body and Blood of Christ—perish the thought!—but the deified Body Itself of the Lord, since the Lord Himself has said: "This is My Body." He did **not** say a type of His Body, **but His Body**; nor a type of His Blood, **but His Blood**...[59]

Thomas Aquinas, Priest, Doctor of the Catholic Church (AD 1225-1274):

> The presence of **Christ's true body and blood** in this sacrament **cannot be detected by sense, nor understanding, but *by faith*** alone, which rests upon Divine authority.[60]

> Yet meanwhile in our pilgrimage **He does not deprive us of His bodily presence**; but **unites us** with Himself in this **sacrament**

[57] William A. Jurgens, *The Faith of the Early Fathers*, Vol. 3 (Collegeville, MN: The Liturgical Press, 1970), 30.
[58] Ibid., 32.
[59] Ibid., 339.
[60] Thomas Aquinas, *Summa Theologica*, Part 3, Question 75, Article 1.

> through the **truth of His body and blood**. Hence (John 6:57) he says: "He that eats My flesh, and drinks My blood, abides in Me, and I in him."[61]

The Lord's Supper is infinitely more than a symbol as taught in most of Protestantism. The *reality* of the Real Presence of Christ in the Eucharist, which was believed by all Christians prior to the Protestant Reformation, proved decisive in my conversion to the apostolic Christian Church! The early Church Fathers stood firmly in unity with this Biblical truth and celebrated the Eucharist as the center of worship—precisely as the apostolic Church continues to do so today!

[61] Thomas Aquinas, *Summa Theologica*, Part 3, Question 75, Paragraph 3.

Chapter 7

The Bible and Sacred Tradition

They devoted themselves to the apostles' teaching,
to the breaking of bread and to prayers.
(Acts of the Apostles 2:42)

✟ What I **discovered** …

Sola scriptura is the Protestant teaching that the Bible alone is the sole rule of faith and authority for Christians. If something is not found written in the Bible, it is excluded from having authority in the life of a Christian. This was my belief for years. Ironically, I discovered *sola scriptura* to be unbiblical, unhistorical, unreasonable, and unworkable! After all, where is it written in the Bible that something must first be written down before it can be believed?

~ 🕮 ~

Catholic Christians, Orthodox Christians, and most Protestant Christians, adamantly affirm and defend the absolute divine inspiration of the written Word of God as the principle record of the Gospel of Jesus Christ. There is agreement that personal spiritual growth through reading, studying, praying, and applying the Bible to our daily life is foundational to following Christ. One early Church Father, Saint Jerome, said: "Ignorance of Scripture is ignorance of Christ!" Catholic Christians, Orthodox Christians, and Protestant Christians further agree that all Scripture is God-breathed (*theopneustos*). The written Word of God, then, is the work of God.

Protestant Fundamentalism and *Sola Scriptura*

The Protestant doctrine of *sola scriptura* teaches that the Bible alone is the sole authority and sole rule of faith for Christians. It teaches that the Bible is self-authenticating as the inspired Word of God. You only need a Bible and the Holy Spirit to guide you to the truth. Doctrines obtained from *sola scriptura* are repeatable, plain, clear, and apparent to people everywhere and at all times. In this framework, Christians should be able to read the Bible under individual guidance of the Holy Spirit and inevitably come to the same conclusions as other *sola scriptura* adherents. Traditions, early Church councils, or any external Biblical authority are not required to reach agreement on the correct interpretation.

The Protestant Bible fundamentalist will certainly ask: "Where is this doctrine or that belief found in the written Word of God?" Others demand a proof text, that is, a verse that shows beyond question the doctrine to be believed (e.g., a smoking gun). The ability to name "chapter and verse" is also a prominent mark of *sola scriptura* and Bible fundamentalism.

While not meant to be an exhaustive treatment of the "Bible alone" theory, what follows will demonstrate the essential tenents as I practiced them in evangelical Protestantism. The Bible teaches that "all Scripture is God-breathed and is useful for teaching, rebuking, correcting, and training in righteousness, so that the servant of God may be thoroughly equipped for every good work" (2 Timothy 3:16-17). Paul declares that the Bible is God-breathed, meaning *divinely inspired.* In the same verse, Paul teaches that the Bible thoroughly equips the man of God for "every good work." I frequently would ask what more is needed if the Bible equips people to do every good work? Why would we need anything else if we can accomplish all the good works that God has called us to do in advance (Ephesians 2:10) by exercising "Bible alone" principles in our daily life?

Protestant theology makes much of the noble Bereans in the Acts of the Apostles. When Paul and Silas were sent away by night to Berea, they arrived at a Jewish synagogue and found that the "Bereans were more noble-minded than the Thessalonians, for they received the message with great eagerness and examined the Scriptures every day to see if these teachings were true" (Acts of the Apostles 17:11). Why were the Bereans "more noble"? They received the message eagerly and "examined the Scriptures every day" to *confirm* the truthfulness of the message. The idea of examining the Scriptures daily seems to support *sola scriptura.*

In the Gospel of Matthew, a group of Pharisees and scribes were testing Jesus. The Pharisees challenged Jesus concerning His disciples breaking the traditions of the elders. Jesus, after some dialogue, responds: "Thus you nullify the word of God by your tradition that you have handed down. And you do many things like that" (Mark 7:13). Jesus, in no uncertain terms, chastises them because they cancel out the Word of God by giving higher praise and honor to man-made, pharisaical traditions. In the Gospel of Matthew, we are told to abandon *traditions of men*. Similarly, Mark's Gospel records that Jesus replied to the Pharisees and teachers of the law by quoting the words of the prophet Isaiah 29:13: "They worship me in vain; their teachings are merely human rules." Jesus tells them, "You have let go of the commands of God and hold on to human traditions" (Mark 7:7-8). How much clearer could Christ be that those people were honoring Him with their lips but their hearts were very far from truly loving and following Him? Thus, more reason to reject worthless *human tradition*.

One Problem: The "Bible Alone" Theory Is *Not* Biblical

As attractive as *sola scriptura* (or, the "Bible Alone" theory) sounds, over time this practice proved to be indefensible, flawed, and unbiblical. Consider the following:[62]

- Is there any Biblical evidence *anywhere* in the New Testament, showing that Jesus intended for His disciples or apostles to *write a book*?
- Did Jesus ever instruct His disciples to produce written accounts of everything they learned and observed while He walked among them?
- Did Jesus command His disciples to distribute books as the primary method of spreading the gospel?

[62] I highly recommend the authoritative, in-depth lecture series by Dr. Scott Hahn entitled *The Bible Alone* (Saint Joseph Communications).

- If Christians are to believe only what is found in *written* Scripture as their sole rule for faith and morals, where does *that belief itself* come from?
- Where in the Bible do we find that something must *first be written* before it can be *believed*?

I invite you to **stop**, **re-read**, and **reflect upon** the previous **5 questions!**

Searching for answers to these questions shook my evangelical Protestant foundation! I began to see profound inconsistencies in *sola scriptura* which persistently begged for a more credible approach to Christian revelation and Church authority. The following facts were instrumental in my journey to see just how unscriptural *sola scriptura* is:

1. The Church existed *prior to* the New Testament.

When Paul wrote his first letter to the church at Corinth in AD 55-56, the Church was *already* in existence:

> Paul, called to be an apostle of Christ Jesus by the will of God, and Sosthenes our brother, **to the church of God that is in Corinth**, to you who have been sanctified in Christ Jesus, called to be holy, with all those everywhere who call upon the name of our Lord Jesus Christ, their Lord and ours. Grace to you and peace from God our Father and the Lord Jesus Christ (1 Corinthians 1:1-3).

This letter to the Corinthians did not exist yet, even though, there was a Church already operating that Paul was writing to. In other words, this very letter in our New Testament was not available to that community in Corinth *until* Paul was led to write to them! In the pastoral letters to Timothy, Paul sends him instructions on worship and Church leadership.

> I am writing you about these matters, although I hope to visit you soon. But if I should be delayed, you should know how to behave in the household of God, which is **the church** of the living God, the pillar and foundation of truth (1 Timothy 3:14-15).

In writing to Timothy, Paul assumes that the Church is *already in existence*. That very Church did *not* have these instructions that Paul was now sending! So the Church at that time would not have known of this part of the Bible we now have, as they were the *recipients* of these instructions. The Church was busy growing and making disciples while parts of the New Testament were still being written.

We read in the Acts of the Apostles that churches throughout Judea began enjoying peace:

> **The church** throughout all Judea, Galilee, and Samaria was at peace. It was being built up and walked in the fear of the Lord, and with the consolation of the Holy Spirit it grew in numbers (Acts of the Apostles 9:31).

How could the Church throughout all Judea, Galilee, and Samaria have been at peace and walking in the Lord with the Holy Spirit without it first having a complete, written New Testament? It is precisely because the Church *existed before* the letters of the New Testament were written! These letters were not written as all-encompassing theological and systematic accounts of Christian doctrine. The New Testament pastoral letters and epistles were written to encourage, correct, or support *existing churches.*

So where does this leave the Protestant doctrine of *sola scriptura* or the "Bible alone" theory? What became of Christians that had no Bible, but, they did have a church? Were they lost and without hope? Henry Grey Graham summarized the logical fallacy of not recognizing that the Bible was written *after* the Church was already in existence.

> What, then, came of those poor souls who lived before the Bible was printed, before it was even written in its present form? How were nations made familiar with the Christian religion and converted to Christianity before the 15th century? Our Divine Lord, I suppose, wished that the unnumbered millions of human creatures born before the year 1500 should believe what He had taught and save their souls and go to Heaven at least as much as those of the 16th and 20th centuries. How could they do this when they had no Bibles, or were too poor to buy one, or could not read it even though they bought it, or

> could not understand it even if they could read it? On the Catholic plan of salvation through the teaching of the Church, souls may be saved and people become saints and believe and do all that Jesus Christ meant them to believe and do. As a matter of fact, this has happened in all countries and in all ages without either the written or the printed Bible, and both before and after its production. The Protestant theory, on the contrary, stakes a man's salvation on the possession of the Bible. This leads to the most flagrant absurdities, imputes to Almighty God a total indifference to the salvation of the countless souls that passed into eternity for 1500 years and indeed ends logically in the blasphemous conclusion that our Blessed Lord failed to provide an adequate means of conveying to men in every age the knowledge of His truth.[63]

2. Jesus did *not* write any Scripture.

It seems only correct to assert that if our Lord desired His followers to focus on a book, He would have mentioned it or alluded to the future development of a written text. Jesus, instead, invests in the lives of the disciples and apostles so that they would build His Church.

[63] Henry G. Graham, *Where We Got the Bible* (Charlotte, NC: TAN Books, 2010), 11-12.

3. The Church, not a written text, is the pillar and foundation of truth.

The Bible says the Church is "the pillar and foundation of the truth" (1 Timothy 3:15). When the apostles began their missions, they did not have a New Testament, but they did have a promise that the Holy Spirit would guide the Church and "bring to remembrance all that He had said and done" (John 14:26) in order to spread the gospel.

The Church, *not* a book, is the "pillar and foundation" of the truth according to the Bible.
(1 Timothy 3:15)

---

4. Jesus *never* commanded His disciples to write books.

Not all of the original Twelve disciples wrote books. If this were the mission of the original Twelve disciples, many of them completely failed! Of course, this shows that their primary mission was not to write a book but to follow Christ and orally preach the gospel, which is exactly what they did through the guidance of the Holy Spirit. Jesus commanded the disciples to go and preach the Good News to the entire world but He never said anything about the disciples writing books.

After the resurrection, the disciples met with Jesus. He sent them out to preach the Good News. They had no books, only His divine authority!

> Then Jesus approached and said to them, "All power in heaven and on earth has

> been given to me. **Go**, therefore, and **make disciples** of all nations, **baptizing them** in the name of the Father, and of the Son, and of the Holy Spirit, **teaching them to observe all that I have commanded you**. And behold, I am with you always, until the end of the age" (Matthew 28:18-20).

Similarly, in Mark's Gospel, Jesus said to go and *preach*:

> He said to them, "**Go** into the whole world and **proclaim the gospel** to every creature…" (Mark 16:15-18).

In Luke's Gospel, Jesus sends out 72 other disciples. They are to speak *on behalf of the Lord Jesus Christ* with *His authority*:

> Whoever **listens to you listens to me**. Whoever **rejects you rejects me**. And whoever rejects me rejects the one who sent me (Luke 10:16).

The Church speaks with the authority of Christ. Returning to Henry G. Graham, he comments:

> Our Blessed Lord Himself never, so far as we know, wrote a line of Scripture—certainly none that has been preserved. He never told His Apostles to write anything. He did not command them to commit to writing what He had delivered to them: but He said, "Go and teach all nations," "Preach the Gospel to every creature," "He that hears you, hears me." What He commanded

> and meant them to do was precisely what He had done Himself, namely, deliver the Word of God to the people by the living voice—convince, persuade, instruct, convert them by addressing themselves face to face to living men and women...[64]

5. The Apostolic Church recognized and compiled the Bible!

The New Testament was written over a period of time from about AD 48 to AD 100. For example, Paul wrote First and Second Thessalonians around AD 51, First Corinthians around AD 55, and Romans around AD 57. Revelation was written by John around AD 90 during his exile on the island of Patmos.

These works existed as separate and distinct writings. However, there were many other letters also claiming to be inspired Scripture. The "canon" (the list of books that make up the Bible) was not finalized for almost 300 years! So, this naturally leads to the question: Which books belong in the Bible? Who recognized which books were of divine origin and which were not? Were early Christians completely lost and without a guide? To the contrary, there was an apostolic Church, established by Christ, even when there was not a completed New Testament Bible in existence!

Athanasius of Alexandria, in his thirty-ninth Festal Letter in AD 367, lists the record of New Testament books we have today. Further, it was not until the Council of Rome in AD 382, the Council of Hippo

[64] Ibid., 18-19.

in AD 393, and Council of Carthage in AD 397 that an approved list of Old Testament and New Testament books was adopted as canonical. In fact, the same list of books was affirmed at a future Council of Carthage held in AD 419. The Catholic Church did not *create* the canon out of her own power. Rather, the canon was *recognized* and *discerned* through the Catholic Church. How is it that Protestantism **must** trust the Catholic Church to recognize and protect the contents of the Bible for over 1,500 years, but throw away everything else the one, holy, catholic, and apostolic Church brought us? Humbly we may ask: Where were Protestant churches when the Catholic Church was busy rejecting all the false "gospels" floating around and assembling the inspired New Testament books into one volume? It is the Catholic Church, and the Holy Spirit working through her bishops, that recognized and formed the Bible we have today.

6. Church authority existed outside of the Bible.

The Council of Jerusalem (AD 49) is particularly instructive with respect to Sacred Scripture and apostolic Tradition. Paul and Timothy "handed on" to the people the "decisions reached by the apostles" which became part of the Christian deposit of faith throughout the world. Churches then grew and became firm in the faith because of the *authoritative decision* made by this Council:

> As they traveled from city to city, they **handed on** to the people for observance the **decisions reached by the apostles** and presbyters in Jerusalem. Day after day

> the **Churches** grew stronger in faith and increased in number (Acts of the Apostles 16:4-5).

The Protestant doctrine of *sola scriptura* could not possibly be applied here, as they did not have Bibles to read and consult for this decision! Yet, they were still able, through *divine authority* and *apostolic succession* given to the Church by Jesus, to make binding decisions which were applicable then and today!

The origin and formation of the Council of Jerusalem, in conjunction with infallible authoritative decisions and subsequent *oral* proclamation of those decisions, is precisely what the Catholic Church has practiced since the time of Christ. Christians who heard final decisions from these councils received them as binding truth. Holy Scripture, Sacred Tradition, and the teaching authority of the Church are plainly evident. Many early Christians placed much importance on the infallibility of Church councils, which were guided by the Holy Spirit. The takeaway here is simply that the Bible was not the only authority for these early Christians.

The Acts of the Apostles records some preachers departing from the *one* Church and going out on their own *without authority*:

> We have heard that some went out from us **without our authorization** and disturbed you, troubling your minds by what they said (Acts of the Apostles 15:24).

These people went out without the apostles' authority! Our Lord prayed for unity in the Church, one body of Christ. God established loving authority to guide it through the sea of time, bringing souls into heaven. Are we like these who have gone out "without authorization" from the Church Jesus established?

7. Faith comes from *hearing* the gospel.

> Faith comes from what is **heard**, and what is **heard** comes through the word of Christ (Romans 10:17).
>
> Now I am reminding you, brothers, of the gospel **I preached** to you, which you indeed received and in which you also stand. Through it you are also being saved, if you **hold** fast **to the word I preached to you**, unless you believed in vain (1 Corinthians 15:1-2).

8. Jesus did many things not recorded in the Bible.

> Now Jesus did many other signs in the presence of his disciples that are **not written in this book** (John 20:30).
>
> There are also many **other things** that Jesus did, but if these were to be described individually, I do not think the whole world would contain the books that would be written (John 21:25).

9. *Sola scriptura* has proven *catastrophic* to Christian unity!

There are over 30,000 different Protestant denominations! Jesus said, "Every good tree bears good fruit, but a bad tree bears bad fruit. A good tree cannot bear bad fruit, and a bad tree cannot bear good fruit. Every tree that does not bear good fruit is cut down and thrown into the fire" (Matthew 7:17-19). Therefore, should we not cut down and discard the unbiblical, unhistorical, and unworkable doctrine of *sola scriptura*? There remains *one*, holy, catholic, and apostolic Church which has been in existence for 2,000 years!

Historically, *sola scriptura* has produced rotten fruits from the time it was introduced. Thousands of competing Protestant denominations have splintered the body of Christ with regrettable consequences.

---

10. Human tradition (secular) vs. Sacred Tradition (apostolic).

Oftentimes, human traditions get in the way of truly connecting with God and His Church. We see this clearly articulated in many situations and stories in the Bible.

> Jesus replied, "And why do you break the command of God for the sake of **your tradition**?" (Matthew 15:3).
>
> Thus you nullify the word of God for the sake of **your tradition** (Matthew 15:6).

> "You have let go of the commands of God and are holding on to **human traditions**." And he continued, "You have a fine way of setting aside the commands of God in order to observe **your own traditions**... Thus you nullify the word of God **by your tradition** that you have handed down. And you do many things like that" (Mark 7:8-9,13).

Conversely, it is also true, that we are commanded to hold on to both Sacred Scripture (the *written* Word of God) **and** Sacred Tradition (*oral* teachings handed down by the apostles):

> So then, brethren, stand firm and **hold to the traditions** which you were taught by us, either by **word of mouth *or* by letter** (2 Thessalonians 2:15).

> I **commend** you because you remember me in everything and **maintain the traditions** even as I have delivered them to you (1 Corinthians 11:2).

> And we also thank God constantly for this, that when you received the Word of God which you **heard from us**, you accepted it **not as the word of men** but as what it really is, **the Word of God**, which is at work in you believers (1 Thessalonians 2:13).

> What you **heard** from me, keep as the pattern of sound **teaching**, with faith and love in Christ Jesus. Guard the **good deposit** that was entrusted to you—**guard**

> **it** with the help of the Holy Spirit who lives in us (2 Timothy 1:13-14).
>
> This is the message we have **heard** from Him and **declare to you**: God is light; in Him there is no darkness at all (1 John 1:5).

Early Christians accepted divine revelation in both forms: *written* Scripture and *oral* Traditions of the apostles, as seen above! *Written* Scripture and *oral* Tradition form *one* deposit of faith. The Magisterium (fancy name for teaching authority of the Church) is not superior to the Word of God, but is the servant of the Word of God!

> The task of giving an authentic interpretation of the Word of God, whether in its written form or in the form of Tradition, has been entrusted to the living, teaching office of the Church alone. Its authority in this matter is exercised in the name of Jesus Christ.... Yet this Magisterium is not superior to the Word of God but its servant. It teaches only what has been handed on to it. At the divine command and with the help of the Holy Spirit, it listens to this devotedly, guards it with dedication, and expounds it faithfully. All that it proposes for belief as being divinely revealed is drawn from this single deposit of faith.[65]

The Holy Spirit, working through the successors and bishops, guards and protects the glorious Gospel

---

[65] CCC, n. 85, 86.

of Jesus from corruption. When Jesus comforted His disciples in John's Gospel, He reminded them not to be troubled, as they would supernaturally be reminded what to teach. They were not bound to a book, but the Holy Spirit working in them through the Church Jesus established. Critical to the point here is the fact that this promise of Jesus is *everlasting.* Nowhere are we *ever* told that when the New Testament is eventually *written*, this promise ceases to be true and disappears. Quite the opposite!

> All this I have spoken while still with you. But the Advocate, the **Holy Spirit**, whom the Father will send in my name, **will teach** you all things and will **remind you of everything I have said to you.** Peace I leave with you; my peace I give you. I do not give to you as the world gives. Do not let your hearts be troubled and do not be afraid (John 14:25-27).

The disciples were *not* acting as scribes or preparing to write books. Rather, they were living out their roles in the Church Jesus established and teaching with the *divine authority* given to them! The exact same thing still happens today in the Catholic Church through apostolic succession.

11. The wisdom of God is not exclusively proclaimed through a book.

It is *through the Church* that the wisdom of God is to be made known!

> His intent was that now, **through the Church, the manifold wisdom of God should be made known** to the rulers and authorities in the heavenly realms, according to his eternal purpose that he accomplished in Christ Jesus our Lord (Ephesians 3:10-11).

12. Some revelation is only known through Sacred Tradition.

There are multiple places (e.g., Jude 8-9) in the New Testament where people or events can only be known through *Sacred Tradition* which is found *outside* of the Bible. An appeal to extrabiblical revelation must be acknowledged. Consider where Paul mentions the names Jannes and Jambres. These two formal names are not mentioned anywhere in the Old Testament. To learn about them, we are forced to consult Tradition.

> Just as **Jannes** and **Jambres** opposed Moses, so they also oppose the truth—people of depraved mind, unqualified in the faith. But they will not make further progress, for their foolishness will be plain to all, as it was with those two (2 Timothy 3:8-9).

Robert A. Sungenis makes the following observation:

> Who are Jannes and Jambres? Well, the Old Testament doesn't mention them, but if you consult a handy Bible reference work, you find they are the Egyptian magicians who opposed Moses. So…if these gentlemen are

> not in the Old Testament, how do Paul (and Timothy) know their names? The same way thousands of their contemporaries knew. For, in fact, Paul is again drawing on (and assuming Timothy will draw on) a widely known extrabiblical *Tradition*, and treating it as authoritative revelation.[66]

2 Timothy 3:16-17
Support for *Sola Scriptura*?

On the surface, this verse seems to support *sola scriptura*, but it actually proves the opposite!

> But as for you, continue in what you have learned and firmly believed, knowing from whom you learned it, and how **from childhood** you have known the sacred writings that are able to instruct you for salvation through faith in Christ Jesus (2 Timothy 3:14-15).

Paul can only be directly referring to the Old Testament. Why? Timothy learned this instruction *from childhood* which implies this verse is referring to the Old Testament, since the New Testament was not yet complete! If Paul was teaching that the Old Testament and a few of the New Testament letters were sufficient *alone* for salvation, it proves too much because then all *later* books become unnecessary!

---

[66] Robert A. Sungenis, Not by Scripture Alone (Santa Barbara, CA: Queenship Publishing, 1997), 179.

> **All Scripture is inspired by God** and is **useful** for teaching, for reproof, for correction, and for training in righteousness, so that everyone who belongs to God may be proficient, **equipped for every good work** (2 Timothy 3:16-17).

Paul never states that Scripture is the *only* source for preparing man for every good work. He does say *every* Scripture, but, not *only* Scripture! Paul was getting ready to journey from this life to heaven. A few verses later, Paul says, "As for me, I am already being poured out as a libation, and the time of my departure has come. I have fought the good fight, I have finished the race, I have kept the faith" (2 Timothy 4:6-7). There is not a *single word* in his exhortation concerning the preparation of a written book. This verse does not explicitly state that Scripture *alone* is all that is required. Remember that we are looking for a verse that declares that Scripture *alone* is the *only* source of authority, not that Scripture is helpful or useful. The former does not exist and all Christians agree on the latter.

Sola 2 Timothy?

Protestant attempts to use 2 Timothy 3 to prove *sola scriptura* inadvertently ignore the book immediately before it! Ironically, in 1 Timothy 3:15, we read that the Church, not a written book, is the "pillar and foundation of truth." I could not help but notice the irony here. While Catholic Christians and Orthodox Christians go by *both* 1 and 2 Timothy, it seems our Protestant brothers go by *sola* 2 Timothy!

The Biblical Evidence

Returning to the questions which began this chapter, we are now able to answer them with certainty. Is there any Biblical evidence, anywhere in the New Testament, showing that Jesus intended for His disciples or apostles to write a book? No. Did Jesus ever instruct His disciples to generate written accounts of everything they observed while He walked among them? No. Did Jesus command His disciples to distribute books as the primary method of spreading the gospel? No. If Christians are to believe only what is found in *the Bible* as their sole rule for faith, where does *this belief* come from? It does not exist in the Bible. *Sola scriptura* falls short on these grounds. There is simply no Biblical basis for it—an ironic conclusion given the nature of the assertion!

Athanasius of Alexandria (AD 295-373):

> Again, we write, again **keeping** to the **apostolic traditions**, we remind each other when we come together for prayer; and keeping the feast in common, with one mouth we truly give thanks to the Lord.[67]

Basil the Great (AD 330-379):

> Of the beliefs and practices that are preserved in the Church, whether generally accepted or publicly enjoined, some we possess derive from **written teaching**; **others** we have received "in a mystery" **by the Tradition of the Apostles**; and **both** of

[67] Philip Schaff, *Nicene and Post-Nicene Fathers*, Series II, Vol. 4, 1256.

> these have the **same force in relation to true religion**... For were we to attempt to reject such customs as have no written authority, on the ground that the importance they possess is small, we should unintentionally injure the gospel in its very vitals; or, rather, should make our public definition a mere phrase and nothing more.[68]

John Chrysostom (died AD 407):

> "So then, brethren, stand fast, and hold the **traditions** that you were taught, whether **by word**, or **by letter** of ours." From this it is manifest that **they did not deliver all things by letter, but many things also unwritten**, and in like manner both the one and the other are worthy of credit. Therefore let us think the **Tradition of the Church** also worthy of credit. It is a Tradition, seek no farther.[69]

Scripture says that the early Christians received both *written* and *oral* apostolic Tradition. As a Protestant, I experienced that when you have a "religion of the book" you end up with chaos, lack of clarity, and disunity—as evidenced in the greater than 30,000 different Protestant denominations all claiming truth. *Sola scriptura* is unscriptural, unhistorical, illogical, incoherent, inconsistent, improbable, and impractical!

---

[68] Basil the Great, *De Spiritu Sancto* (of the Holy Spirit), Chapter 27:66.

[69] John Chrysostom, *Homilies on Second Thessalonians*, IV, Ver. 15.

Yet, I discovered that when you have a living authority, passed down from the apostles, you have clarity, uniformity, and unity of doctrine! As a member of the one, holy, Catholic, and apostolic Church, I have experienced profound unity reaching back to the apostles, and thus, Christ.

Chapter 8

Mary, the Mother of Our Lord

Jesus said to the disciple, "Behold, your mother."
And from that hour the disciple took her into his home.
(John 19:27)

✞ What I **discovered** ...

The mention of the Blessed Virgin Mary stirs up warm contemplation in the hearts of most Christians. In contrast, the Protestant fundamentalist often reacts with deep skepticism. Regardless, the Biblical reality of the Virgin Mary in salvation history is stunning. Mary is prefigured from the beginning in Genesis. She actively participates with Christ in the Gospels and is observed fighting Satan in Revelation! The four dogmas taught by the apostolic Church (Immaculate Conception, Perpetual Virginity, Assumption, and Mary as the Mother of God) bring Christians into a closer relationship with her Son, our Lord and Savior Jesus Christ. While Mary is honored in apostolic Christianity, she is not worshipped.

Mary, the First Disciple

In Luke, the angel Gabriel appeared to Mary and told her she would give birth to Jesus. Mary responds in obedience and surrenders her will to God:

> Mary said, "Behold, I am the handmaid of the Lord. May it be done to me according to your word" (Luke 1:38).

In what is called *The Magnificat*, we find Mary offering a glorious hymn of praise to almighty God:

> My soul proclaims the greatness of the Lord;
> my spirit rejoices in God my savior.
> For he has looked upon his handmaid's lowliness;
> behold, from now on will all ages *call me blessed.*
> The Mighty One has done great things for me,
> and holy is his name.
> His mercy is from age to age
> to those who fear him.
> He has shown might with his arm,
> dispersed the arrogant of mind and heart.
> He has thrown down the rulers from their thrones
> but lifted up the lowly.
> The hungry he has filled with good things;
> the rich he has sent away empty.
> He has helped Israel his servant,
> remembering his mercy,
> According to his promise to our fathers,
> to Abraham and to his descendants forever.
> (Luke 1:46-55)

The Magnificat is inspiring. Mary's praise to God should greatly encourage us to *imitate* her example! The Bible says that all generations will call Mary "blessed." Catholic and Orthodox Christians do, but, it begs the question: Why don't Protestants? Immediately, we see Mary as a model disciple. However, what about Catholic doctrines, such as the Immaculate Conception and

Perpetual Virginity of Mary? How are these Biblical? To best answer these questions, we turn to the apostolic Christian understanding of *typology*.

Just My *Type*!

Typology, the study of types, is extremely helpful in understanding relationships that exist between the New Testament and the Old Testament. A *type* is a person or event in the Old Testament that prefigures or foreshadows a reality in the New Testament. The early Christian theologian Augustine recognized this relationship: The New Testament lies hidden in the Old and the Old Testament is unveiled in the New.[70] Many Christian doctrines are best understood in the framework of typological relationships. Doctrines related to Mary, and her place in salvation history, are highlighted through the careful study of typology.

Jesus is the *New Adam*

Paul says that Adam is a *type* of Christ.

> But death reigned from Adam to Moses, even over those who did not sin after the pattern of the trespass of Adam, who is **the type** of the one who was to come (Romans 5:14).

From Paul's description, we can see how Jesus is the New Adam. Recall, in the first Adam, all people die through sin. In the New Adam, many are made alive! Jesus came to undo what Adam did.

[70] Augustine, CCC, n. 129.

> For just as through the **disobedience of one** person the many were **made sinners**, so through the **obedience of one** the many will be **made righteous** (Romans 5:19).

Paul reflects on the typological relationship between the first Adam and the New Adam. Here, Paul affirms that human sin is inherited from Adam but Christ brings freedom and deliverance.

> For since death came through a human being, the resurrection of the dead came also through a human being. For just as **in Adam all die**, so too **in Christ shall all be brought to life** (1 Corinthians 15:21-22).

To further illustrate the typological relationship pointing to Jesus as the New Adam, consider the following:

Adam was a *sinner…*	New Adam (Jesus) was *sinless.*
Adam brought *death…*	New Adam brought *life.*
Adam brought *darkness…*	New Adam brought *light.*
Adam was *disobedient…*	New Adam was *obedient.*
Adam *brought a curse…*	New Adam *reversed the curse.*
Adam brought *judgment…*	New Adam brought *salvation.*
Adam was born *from dust…*	New Adam was born *from heaven.*

> So, too, it is written, "The **first man, Adam**, became a living being," the **last Adam** a life-giving spirit. But the spiritual was

> not first; rather the natural and then the spiritual. The first man was from the **earth**, earthly; the second man, from **heaven** (1 Corinthians 15:45-47).

Mary is the *New Eve*

Now, consider Eve and Mary. Irenaeus, in the second century explains, "the knot of Eve's *disobedience* was loosed by the *obedience* of Mary." Irenaeus further articulates, "For what the virgin Eve had *bound* fast through *unbelief*, this did the virgin Mary *set free* through *faith*."[71] Likewise, Jerome, in the fourth century, understood the connection between Eve and Mary. He wrote, "Death came through Eve, but life has come through Mary."[72] Like the New Adam, we can see that Mary is the New Eve through a similar contrast:

Eve gave birth to *death*…	New Eve (Mary) gave birth to *Life*.
Eve gave birth to *sin*…	New Eve gave birth to *grace*.
Eve listened to the *serpent*…	New Eve listened to the *angel*.
Eve was *disobedient* to God…	New Eve was *obedient* to God.
Eve is the mother of *all living*…	New Eve is the mother to *all spiritually alive*.

The Biblical data is clear: Jesus is the *New Adam* and Mary is the *New Eve*.

[71] Irenaeus, *Against Heresies* (Beloved Publishing, 2015), 287.
[72] Letters of St. Jerome, Letter 22, 21.

The *Woman* Prefigured in Genesis

Prefigure means to imagine, or represent, someone or something beforehand. In Genesis, there is an absolutely stunning prophecy made by God. After Adam and Eve originally sinned, God spoke concerning enmity (opposition, hostility) that would be perpetually established between the *woman* and the serpent.

> I will put **enmity** between **you** and the **woman**, and between your offspring and hers. **He will crush your head** and **you will strike his heel** (Genesis 3:15).

This passage in Genesis is called the *Protoevangelium* (first gospel): the first announcement of the Messiah and Redeemer, of a battle between the serpent and the Woman, and of the final victory of a descendant of hers.[73] This is the first announcement of a Savior and a foreshadowing or prefiguring of Mary!

The question is: Who crushed the head of the serpent? We know this can only be Jesus. Jesus is the seed or offspring of this woman. Jesus crushed the head of Satan at the Cross of Calvary. Astonishingly, the site of Calvary in which Jesus defeated Satan means "skull-place" reminiscent of crushing Satan's head. Because Jesus is the seed or offspring of the woman, who must the woman be? Mary! She is prefigured right here in the beginning of Genesis! It is interesting that Adam and Eve ushered in sin and death, but Mary (the "New Eve") and Jesus (the "New Adam") bring salvation, redemption, and freedom to mankind. It is also vital to recognize that *only* Jesus can bring salvation and free

---

[73] CCC, n. 410.

us from sin. Yet, God used Mary as an instrument for His work to redeem mankind. In this *sense*, Jesus and Mary "work together" to bring salvation to the ends of the earth through her Son Jesus. Many Christian paintings, icons, and images depict Mary with her foot on the head of a snake!

> Mary is *prefigured* in Genesis. It is her offspring, Jesus, who defeats Satan.

The *Woman* at the Wedding

At the wedding at Cana in Galilee, Jesus replies to Mary, "Dear *woman*, why do you involve me?" (John 2:4). Protestant theology suggests this is a harsh response from Jesus. However, from the typology examined above, we understand that the reference *woman* is not to be taken in any sense derogatory. This response, *woman*, is a natural reference back to the prefigured Mary in Genesis!

The *Woman* at the Cross of Calvary

A related reference is found in John's account of the crucifixion. Mary stood near the Cross as Jesus said to her, "Dear *woman*, here is your *son,*" and to the disciple, "Here is your *mother*" (John 19:26-27). Mary was *not* John's biological mother, yet John is called Mary's son, and Mary, John's *mother*! This Biblical account presented a dilemma for me as an evangelical Protestant, for in my mind, Mary could never be anyone's mother who was not biological; yet, this is precisely what Scripture says. This creates uneasy implications for the Protestant who insists we should never call Mary *mother*. The Bible says Mary became the *mother* of John. Thus, it becomes easy to see that Mary may also be our spiritual *mother* just as she was for John!

Are *You* Like the Beloved Disciple?

The beloved disciple is a model which must be true of *all* disciples of Jesus, including me and you! The disciple whom Jesus loved took Mary into his home and became a spiritual son to her. Equally, Mary became the spiritual *mother* of the beloved disciple. Christians following the model discipleship of the "disciple whom Jesus loved" should ask: Am I like the beloved disciple by taking Mary into my home? When we consider how this disciple was faithful in obeying the command of Jesus to receive Mary as his *mother*, it becomes natural to do likewise!

The *Woman* in Revelation

In Revelation, we find another exciting connection verifying Mary as the *woman* and spiritual *mother* of Christians:

> Then the dragon became angry with *the woman* and went off to wage war against the rest of *her offspring*, those who keep God's commandments and *bear witness to Jesus* (Revelation 12:17).

Eve is the mother of all earthly living people, while Mary is the spiritual *mother* of all people who follow her son Jesus (like John). The *woman* in Revelation has other children in the sense that they are those who keep the commandments of God and "bear testimony to Jesus" (Christians).

Jesus calls Mary the *mother* of John. Later, John calls Mary the *mother* of all Christians. This provides Scriptural support for the Christian acknowledgment of Mary as our *spiritual* mother and mother of the Church.

The *Woman* Clothed with the Sun

John wrote about a *woman* and a child in Revelation that captured my attention for years. Who exactly is the *woman*? Who is the *woman* clothed with the sun? Is she the Church, Mary, or Israel?

> Then God's temple in heaven was opened, and the ark of his covenant could be seen in the temple. There were flashes of lightning, rumblings, and peals of thunder, an earthquake, and a violent hailstorm. A great sign appeared in the sky, a **woman** clothed with the sun, with the moon under her feet, and on her head a crown of twelve stars. She was **with child** and wailed aloud in pain as she labored to give birth. Then another sign appeared in the sky; it was a huge red dragon, with seven heads and ten horns, and on its heads were seven diadems. Its tail swept away a third of the stars in the sky and hurled them down to the earth. Then the dragon stood before the **woman about to give birth**, to devour **her**

> **child** when she gave birth. She gave birth to a **son, a male child**, destined to **rule all the nations** with an **iron rod. Her child** was caught up to **God and his throne** (Revelation 11:19-12:5).

The *woman* has a male child who is destined to rule all the nations, an obvious reference to Jesus and His Kingship! Jesus was caught up to heaven which is what apostolic Christianity calls the Ascension of our Lord Jesus Christ. The *woman* is, therefore, undoubtedly Mary! For completeness, the *woman* could also refer to the Church and Israel. In Catholic theology all of these are valid.

> We can see here that "the woman" described in Rev. 12 can, indeed, refer to the Blessed Virgin Mary, assumed into heaven body and soul, who can, at the same time, embody a collective group of people (the people of Israel and/or the Christian Church). Early Christians such as St. Epiphanius of Salamis (circa 375 AD) Quodvultdeus (circa 450 AD) and Andrew of Caeserea (circa 550 AD) saw this "woman" in heaven as the Blessed Virgin Mary, assumed into heaven body and soul, with her Son, Jesus.[74]

The *Catholic Commentary on Sacred Scripture* reinforces this interpretation:

> When the entire text is taken into account the woman is seen to be faithful Israel,

---

[74] Fr. Mario P. Romero, *Unabridged Christianity* (Goleta, CA: Queenship Publishing, 1999), 279.

> personalized as daughter Zion, who gives birth to the Messiah. As the same, the woman is the literal mother of the Messiah, Mary of Nazareth. Finally, the woman is the Church, whom God cares for during her time in the wilderness of this world and who brings forth other children (12:17). This vision illustrates Revelation's symbolic way of communicating, the multiple levels of meaning in its images, and the book's nonlinear chronology, since the story that this vision tells begins before the birth of Christ.[75]

Mary is the Ark of the *New* Covenant

In the Old Testament, the Ark of the Covenant is described in Exodus as being covered with gold. Likewise, the New Testament describes the Ark of the Covenant as gold covered:

> Have them make a chest of acacia wood... overlay it with **pure gold, both inside and out**... Cast four gold rings for it... then make poles of acacia wood and overlay them with gold (Exodus 25:10-13).
>
> Behind the second curtain was a room called the Most Holy Place, which had the golden altar of incense and the **gold-covered Ark of the Covenant** (Hebrews 9:3-4).

[75] Peter S. Williamson, *Catholic Commentary on Sacred Scripture* (Grand Rapids, MI: Baker Academic, 2015), 210.

Notice how the Ark of the Covenant is covered with *pure gold,* both *inside* and *out.* Gold is associated with holiness, purity, and consecration to God. This directly *foreshadows* the purity, holiness, and consecration to God of the Ark of the *New* Covenant, the Virgin Mary!

The Ark of the Covenant held three items:

> This ark contained the gold jar of **manna**, **Aaron's staff** that had budded, and the **stone tablets** of the covenant (Hebrews 9:4).

First, there were stone tablets containing the Commandments given to Moses. Second, the rod belonging to Aaron, who personified a priestly office, was present. Third, the Bread of Heaven (manna) which fed the Israelites was inside. The Ark of the Covenant can be described as a pure or spotless enclosure holding bread, the word of God, and a priestly staff.

Compare the Ark of the Covenant with the Virgin Mary. What was contained *inside* Mary? The Word of God, our great High Priest, and the Bread of Heaven, which are analogous to the contents inside the Ark of the Covenant!

Ark of the Covenant:	**Ark of the *New* Covenant (Mary):**
was made from *pure gold...*	was created *pure and holy.*
carried the *word of God...*	carried the *Word of God*/ Jesus.
carried the *high priest's staff...*	carried our *High Priest*/Jesus.
carried the *bread of heaven...*	carried the *Bread of Heaven*/ Jesus.

How can the *ark* of the Lord come to me? (2 Samuel 6:9).	Why is this granted me, that the *mother of my Lord* should come to me? (Luke 1:43).
The *ark of the Lord remained* in the house of Obed-edom… (2 Samuel 6:10).	*Mary remained* in the house of Elizabeth… (Luke 1:56).
Ark stayed for *three months* (2 Samuel 6:11).	Mary stayed for *three months* (Luke 1:56).
The Holy Spirit *overshadowed the ark* (Exodus 40:34-35).	The Holy Spirit *overshadowed Mary* (Luke 1:35).

The Holy Spirit "overshadowed" the Ark of the Covenant, bringing God's presence to the people! In the New Testament, we find that the Ark of the *New* Covenant, Mary, was likewise "overshadowed" with the Holy Spirit. As with the Ark of the Covenant, which perpetuated special graces to the people, the Ark of the *New* Covenant (Mary) also perpetuates graces to the followers of her Son Jesus!

Through Biblical typology, we quickly realize how Mary, the Ark of the *New* Covenant, must have also been kept pure and holy by the grace of God. The womb of Mary was the New Ark that carried Jesus, the Word of God, for nine months. This is precisely the Catholic doctrine of the Immaculate Conception of Mary!

The Immaculate Conception

The Ark of the Covenant was created pure, inside and out, set aside for a divine purpose. Mary, the Ark of the *New* Covenant, was likewise preserved, pure and spotless, for a divine purpose.

As I discovered, the Catholic teaching is precisely this: Mary from the first moment of her conception, by a special grace and privilege from Jesus Christ, was preserved from sin because of her special mission. Does this mean Mary did not need a Savior? Of course she did, but the work of Christ transcends time. For example, consider this analogy:

> Suppose a man falls into a deep pit, and someone reaches down to pull him out. The man has been "saved" from the pit. Now imagine a woman walking along, and she too is about to topple into the pit, but at the very moment that she is to fall in, someone holds her back and prevents her. She too has been saved from the pit, but in an even better way: She was not simply taken out of the pit; she was prevented from getting stained by the mud in the first place...By receiving Christ's grace at her conception, she had his grace applied to her before she was able to become mired in original sin and its stain.[76]

Mary's Immaculate Conception is more a statement about Jesus than about Mary. It proclaims that Jesus is so unique and holy that God would even prepare His mother for His birth by preserving her from sin. Thus, it is no surprise to find Saint Ephrem's hymn from AD 370:

---

[76] *The Essential Catholic Survival Guide* (San Diego, CA: Catholic Answers Press, 2005), 127-128.

> You alone and your mother are more beautiful than any others. For there is no blemish in you, nor any stains upon your mother. Who of my children can compare in beauty to these…

Perpetual Virginity

The Ark of the Covenant was never to be touched by sinful man (2 Samuel 6:1-9). Likewise, the Ark of the *New* Covenant (Mary) was never to be touched by sinful man.

"Doesn't the Bible say Jesus had brothers and sisters?"

Mary's Perpetual Virginity is firmly established through Biblical typology. Mary *is* the Ark of the *New* Covenant. Yet, there are verses in Scripture that appear to indicate the opposite. For example, Matthew 12:46-50, Mark 6:3, John 7:5, Acts 1:14, and 1 Corinthians 9:5 mention the "brothers" of Jesus, apparently indicating Mary was not a perpetual virgin. When I was a Protestant, I assumed "brother" always demanded a biological relationship. However, upon deeper study of Scripture, I discovered the Biblical reasons why early Christians and the apostolic Church believe and teach the doctrine of the Perpetual Virginity of Mary.

1. There is not a word for "cousin" in ancient Hebrew or Aramaic. Thus, Jews used "brother" generically, which can include "cousin," "nephew," or "uncle." For example, in the Old Testament, we find that Lot is called Abram's "brother":

> And when Abram heard that his **brother** was taken captive, he armed his trained servants, born in his own house, three hundred and eighteen, and pursued them unto Dan (Genesis 14:14).

However, in Genesis 11:27 we read that Lot is Abram's nephew, ***not his biological brother!***

2. In the New Testament, we read of four men who are called "brothers" of Jesus:

> Is not this the carpenter's son? Is not his mother called Mary? And are not his **brothers** James and Joseph and Simon and Judas? (Matthew 13:55).

In the same Gospel, we read about a group of women with Jesus at the Cross:

> There were many women there, looking on from a distance, who had followed Jesus from Galilee, ministering to him. Among them were Mary Magdalene and Mary the mother of James and Joseph, and the mother of the sons of Zebedee (Matthew 27:55-56).

Continuing the story, we read:

> Mary Magdalene was there, and the other Mary, sitting opposite the grave (Matthew 27:61).

The "other Mary" is not the Virgin Mary, but is the mother of James and Joseph. In addition, we find further support in John's account of the crucifixion:

> Standing by the cross of Jesus were His mother, and His mother's sister, Mary the *wife* of Clopas, and Mary Magdalene (John 19:25).

The women at the Cross are the Virgin Mary, her sister Mary (wife of Clopas), and Mary Magdalene. Interestingly, Mary (the wife of Clopas) is identified as the Mary in Matthew's Gospel, which is the mother of James and Joseph. A striking point here is that this Mary is *not* the wife of Joseph, but of Clopas! Therefore, Joseph and James are ***not the biological brothers of Jesus!***

3. James, the Lord's "brother" is often cited in an attempt to show Jesus had biological siblings:

> Then three years later I went up to Jerusalem to become acquainted with Cephas, and stayed with him fifteen days. But I did not see any other of the apostles except James, the Lord's **brother** (Galatians 1:18-19).

It is important to note that this James, the "brother" of Jesus, is identified as an *apostle*, one of the Twelve. When reviewing the names of the Apostles, we find two Jameses: one had a father named Zebedee; the other had a father named Alphaeus.

> Jesus called his twelve disciples to him and gave them authority to drive out impure spirits and to heal every disease and sickness. These are the names of the twelve apostles: first, Simon (who is called Peter) and his brother Andrew; *James son of Zebedee*, and his brother John; Philip and Bartholomew;

> Thomas and Matthew the tax collector; *James son of Alphaeus*, and Thaddaeus; Simon the Zealot and Judas Iscariot, who betrayed him (Matthew 10:1-4).

Neither one of these Jameses have Joseph as their father. Therefore ***they are not biological brothers of Jesus!***

4. There are subtle hints in Scripture that give more information. For example, consider this passage in the Gospel of Mark:

> Is not this the carpenter, **the son** of Mary, and brother of James and Joses and Judas and Simon? Are not His sisters here with us? (Mark 6:3).

Why is Jesus called "the son" of Mary, not "a son"?

5. The Protestant fundamentalist belief that the word "brothers" always implies *biological* relationships leads to error. For example, Luke records the following:

> They all joined together constantly in prayer, along with the women and Mary the mother of Jesus, and with his **brothers**. In those days Peter stood up among the believers (a group numbering about a hundred and twenty) and said, "**Brothers** and sisters, the Scripture had to be fulfilled in which the Holy Spirit spoke long ago through David concerning Judas, who served as guide for those who arrested Jesus" (Acts 1:14-16).

Are we to believe that because these people are referred to as "brothers" that a woman gave birth to over 80 *biological* children? Obviously, they ***are not biological brothers***. Likewise, we find the following narrative:

> After that, he (Christ) appeared to more than five hundred of the **brothers** and sisters at the same time, most of whom are still living, though some have fallen asleep (1 Corinthians 15:6).

Are we to believe Mary has over 500 children? Obviously there are different meanings for "brother" and ***these are not biological brothers!***

6. Scripture says that before Jesus died, He entrusted His mother to the beloved disciple, John.

> When Jesus then saw His mother, and the disciple whom He loved standing nearby, He said to His mother, "Woman, behold, your son!" Then He said to the disciple, "Behold, your mother!" From that hour the disciple took her into his own *household* (John 19:26-27).

This would have been a major violation of the Jewish family covenant and customs if John was entrusted with the care of Mary, instead of *biological siblings,* who were allegedly standing right next to them. Would Jesus break up His family this way? On the other hand, if Mary did not have other sons, it would make perfect sense to entrust her to the Apostle John!

7. In the Gospel of Luke, Jesus uses the term "brothers" not in a biological and literal way but a spiritual way. In this case, ***they are not biological brothers!***

> And His mother and **brothers** came to Him, and they were unable to get to Him because of the crowd. And it was reported to Him, "Your mother and Your brothers are standing outside, wishing to see You." But He answered and said to them, "My mother and My **brothers** are these who hear the word of God and do it" (Luke 8:19-21).

8. Jesus says that we are to call each other "brothers." Clearly we are ***not biological brothers*** despite referring to one another as "brothers."

> But you are not to be called "Rabbi," for you have one Teacher, and you are **all brothers** (Matthew 23:8).

9. We find a similar statement in Mark's Gospel. Jesus calls people "brothers" and "sisters" who do His will. Again, these people ***are not biological brothers or sisters!***

> Whoever does God's will is my **brother** and **sister** and mother (Mark 3:35).

10. The Apostle Paul refers to Timothy as his brother:

> Paul, an apostle of Christ Jesus by the will of God, and Timothy our **brother**, To God's holy people in Colossae, the faithful brothers and sisters in Christ: Grace

> and peace to you from God our Father (Colossians 1:1-2).
>
> We sent Timothy, who is our **brother** and co-worker in God's service in spreading the gospel of Christ, to strengthen and encourage you in your faith... (1 Thessalonians 3:2).
>
> I want you to know that our **brother** Timothy has been released. If he arrives soon, I will come with him to see you (Hebrews 13:23).

Clearly Timothy was a spiritual brother, ***not a biological brother!***

11. The Church Fathers and early Christians in the second, third, fourth, and fifth century, consistently spoke of the Perpetual Virginity of Mary (e.g., "Ever Virgin"). Origen of Alexandria (AD 249), Athanasius of Alexandria (AD 295-373), Ambrose Bishop of Milan (AD 338-397), Jerome (AD 383), Augustine Bishop of Hippo (AD 354-430), Cyril of Alexandria (AD 430), and Pope Leo the Great (died AD 461) all attest to Mary's Perpetual Virginity!

12. The Protestant Reformation leaders I looked to for Biblical teaching believed the Perpetual Virginity of Mary. Martin Luther, John Calvin, and Ulrich Zwingli all accepted and believed this doctrine. I found it odd that Protestants today break from the faith of their very own founders!

13. The term "brother" does not always mean a biological brother. Likewise, "fathers" are not always biological fathers. For example:

> They said, "Is this not Jesus, the son of Joseph, whose *father* and mother we know? How can he now say, 'I came down from heaven'?" (John 6:42).

Did you catch that? Joseph is called the "father" of Jesus. However, ***Joseph is not the biological father of Jesus!***

14. Today, Christians often call each other "brother and sister" in Christ. We understand that we are ***not biological siblings.*** Amen, brother? Amen, sister?

Mary's Role in Spiritual Battles

The Ark of the Covenant went before the people in battle. In this way, the Ark of the Covenant *assisted* in overcoming the enemies of Israel and helped to secure victory (e.g., the battle of Jericho). The Ark of the Covenant and God's presence was a powerful weapon and protection. Turning to Mary, the Ark of the *New* Covenant, we now understand how she is likewise a weapon in our spiritual battles! This connection is further strengthened in Revelation 11-12.

Honor Your Mother!

In Luke's Gospel, the angel Gabriel, sent by God, announces:

> *Hail Mary,* ***full of grace****, the Lord is with thee* (Luke 1:28).

Gabriel had no hesitation in greeting Mary with *honor*. But, wait a minute! Doesn't the angel Gabriel offer *honor* to Mary when that honor should have been given to God *alone*? Apparently, the angel from God did not have any reservations about *honoring* Mary!

Honoring Mary

The angel sent by God honored Mary. We honor special people every day. Jesus honored his mother and father. Catholic Christians honor Mary but *never* worship her.

We honor our soldiers. We honor our mother and father, as this is a commandment. One would never claim that this type of honor takes away from honor that belongs to God alone. Surely, Jesus honored His mother and father! How fitting it is to honor the Mother of God, as Christ did. We give honor to saints in the family of God *without* worshipping them. God *alone* is to be worshipped. This is the teaching of the apostolic Church and has been for 2,000 years.

Jesus calls us His brothers (Hebrews 2:11-12). Paul explains that Christians are spiritual members of the *one* body of Christ (1 Corinthians 12:27). Since the members of the Church are spiritual brothers to Jesus, and Mary is the mother of Christ, it follows that Mary is our spiritual mother. You cannot have Jesus as your brother without Mary as your mother. Therefore, how should Christians see Mary?

A Walk through the *Biblical* Hail Mary Prayer

As an evangelical Protestant, prayers such as the "Hail Mary" seemed like man-made traditions. Is the "Hail Mary" prayer Biblical?

"Hail Mary, full of grace, the Lord is with thee"

This greeting is taken directly from the Bible! Recall the angel Gabriel's greeting to Mary found in Luke's Gospel: "And he came to her and said, 'Hail, full of grace, the Lord is with thee!'" (Luke 1:28). The salutation by a messenger of God starts with "Hail" which is an honorary title given to a person in a royal position; for example, "Hail Caesar" or "Hail, Holy Queen." Mary is certainly in a special position as she is selected to carry the Son of God! Some translations, especially modern Protestant Bibles, might use the words "Hail, favored one" or "You who are highly favored!" An angel graces Mary with a special greeting that simply means Mary is *set apart* for a divine purpose, a unique role in salvation history. The Lord is indeed with Mary. In the angel's greeting to Mary, "Hail, full of grace," the Greek perfect passive participle *kecharitomene* is used. This indicates Mary *has been* filled with grace. Thus, Mary *has been,* and *is,* filled with grace! The action implies perpetual grace, an important truth in understanding the Immaculate Conception of Mary.

"Blessed art thou among women and blessed is the Fruit of thy womb"

This blessing, too, is taken directly from the Bible! Elizabeth's statement is a blessing to Mary given that she is carrying Jesus within her womb! In Luke, we read, "Most blessed are you among women, and blessed is the fruit of your womb" (Luke 1:42).

"Holy Mary"

"Holy" and "blessed" can be used interchangeably. The Bible declares that Mary will be called blessed in all generations: "for he has looked with favor on the lowliness of his servant. Surely, from now on all generations will call me blessed" (Luke 1:48).

"Mother of God"

The title "Mother of God" was used and believed by Cyril, Ambrose, Jerome, and most early Christians. Elizabeth, John the Baptist's mother, exclaimed, "And how does this happen to me, that the *mother of my Lord* should come to me?" (Luke 1:43). Elizabeth recognizes that Mary is the mother of God. Is Jesus God? Was Mary carrying Jesus in her womb? Did Mary give birth to Jesus? It's not hard to see that Mary is the "Mother of God." The earliest Christians referred to Mary as *Theotokos*, a Greek word meaning "God-bearer." Jesus has two natures, fully human and fully divine. These natures are entirely united, without any division. Since Mary is the mother of Jesus, Mary is appropriately called the "Mother of God." It is no wonder the early Church Father, Irenaeus, writes: "The Virgin Mary… being obedient to His word, received from an angel the glad tidings that she would **bear God**."

"Pray for us sinners now and at the hour of our death." Amen.

The Bible teaches that Christians are to intercede for each other. The body of Christ is both on earth and in heaven. There is only *one* body of Christ! Paul says, "I urge, then, first of all, that petitions, prayers, intercession, and thanksgiving be made for *all people*" (1 Timothy 2:1). Thus, asking for prayer, through petitions and intercession, is Biblical and even commanded. Intercessory prayer is discussed in great detail in the next chapter on communion of the saints. For now, we recognize every verse in the "Hail Mary" prayer as being firmly Biblical.

Martin Luther on Mary— He *really* believed that?

Perhaps most shocking for me, as a Protestant Christian, was the historical fact that many of the very *founders* of Protestant Christianity believed numerous apostolic teachings about Mary. Martin Luther (1483-1546) was the *founder* of the Protestant Reformation, yet, he maintained Mary was the "Mother of God," believed in the Perpetual Virginity (Ever Virgin), and the Immaculate Conception of Mary! Martin Luther was a Catholic priest and monk before he decided to break from the apostolic Church. One might expect he would have rejected the Church's teachings about the Virgin Mary, but the opposite is true.

Martin Luther on Mary as the "Mother of God":

> She is rightly called not only the mother of the man, but also the **Mother of God** ... It is certain that Mary is the **Mother of the real and true God**...[77]

[77] *Luther's Works*, Vol. 24, 107.

Martin Luther on Mary's Perpetual Virginity:

> Christ...was the only Son of Mary, and the **Virgin Mary bore no children besides him**...[78]

Martin Luther on Mary's Immaculate Conception:

> In the first place, she is full of grace, proclaimed to be **entirely without sin**—something exceedingly great. For God's grace fills her with everything good and makes her devoid of all evil... Moreover, God **guarded** and **protected** her from all that might be hurtful to her.[79]

A Protestant's Dilemma

Protestants are left to wiggle on the horns of a very sharp dilemma. If you are a Lutheran, Methodist, or Baptist, chances are that you reject the Perpetual Virginity and Immaculate Conception of Mary. However, *the very founder of Protestantism* believed the Perpetual Virginity and the Immaculate Conception of Mary. I found myself at a serious crossroad. My Protestant church rejected these teachings on Mary, while the founder of Protestantism faithfully believed apostolic Church teachings on Mary. Should I believe my Protestant pastor or Martin Luther? The radical departure of Protestant churches from even their own founders on these teachings, and others, displays just

---

[78] *Luther's Works*, Vol. 22, 214.

[79] *Luther's Works*, Vol. 43, 40.

how distant Protestantism has become from what was handed down from the apostles.

What the Church Fathers and Early Christians Believed About the Blessed Virgin Mary.

***Perpetual Virginity*:**

Athanasius of Alexandria (AD 295-373)

> Therefore let those who deny that the Son is from the Father by nature and proper to His Essence, deny also that He took true human flesh of **Mary Ever-Virgin**.[80]

Jerome (AD 383)

> You say that Mary did not continue a virgin: I claim still more, that Joseph himself on account of Mary was a virgin, so that from a virgin wedlock a virgin son was born. For if as a holy man he does not come under the imputation of fornication, and it is nowhere written that he had another wife, but was the guardian of Mary whom he was supposed to have to wife rather than her husband, the conclusion is that he who was thought worthy to be called father of the Lord, remained a virgin.[81]

Ambrose Bishop of Milan (AD 338-397)

> Imitate [Mary], holy mothers, who in her only dearly beloved Son set forth so great

---

[80] Discourse 2 Against the Arians, n. 70.

[81] Jerome, *The Perpetual Virginity of Blessed Mary, Against Helvidius*, AD 383.

an example of maternal virtue; for **neither have you** sweeter children, **nor did the Virgin seek the consolation of being able to bear another son.**[82]

Augustine Bishop of Hippo (AD 354-430)

Thus Christ by being born of **a virgin, who, before she knew Who was to be born of her, had determined to continue a virgin**, chose rather to approve, than to command, holy virginity. And thus, even in the female herself, in whom He took the form of a servant, He willed that virginity should be free.[83]

Pope Leo the Great (died AD 461)

The origin is different but the nature like: not by intercourse with man but by the power of God was it brought about: for a Virgin conceived, a Virgin bare, and **a Virgin she remained.**

***Immaculate Conception*:**

Ephraim (died AD 373)

You alone and your Mother are more beautiful than any others; For there is **no blemish** in you, **nor any stains upon our**

[82] Philip Schaff, *Nicene and Post-Nicene Fathers*, Series II, Vol. 10.

[83] Philip Schaff, *Nicene and Post-Nicene Fathers*, Series I, Vol. 3.

> **Mother**. Who of my children can compare in beauty to these?[84]

Ambrose Bishop of Milan (AD 338-397)

> Lift me up not from Sara but from Mary, a Virgin not only undefiled but a Virgin whom grace has made inviolate, **free of every stain of sin**.[85]

Augustine Bishop of Hippo (AD 354-430)

> We must except the holy Virgin Mary, concerning whom I wish to raise no question when it touches the subject of sins, out of honor to the Lord; for from Him we know what abundance of grace for overcoming sin in every particular was conferred upon her who had the merit to conceive and bear Him who undoubtedly had no sin.[86]

***Mary, the Mother of God*:**

Cyril of Jerusalem (AD 350)

> The Father bears witness from heaven to his Son. The Holy Spirit bears witness, coming down in the form of a dove. The archangel Gabriel bears witness, bringing the good

---

[84] William A. Jurgens, *The Faith of the Early Fathers*, Vol. 1, The Nisibene Hymns, 27, 8, #719, p. 313.

[85] William A. Jurgens, *The Faith of the Early Fathers*, Vol. 2 [22, 30], #1314, p. 166.

[86] Philip Schaff, *Nicene and Post-Nicene Fathers*, Series II, Vol. 5.

> tidings to Mary. The Virgin **Mother of God** bears witness.[87]

Ambrose Bishop of Milan (AD 338-397)

> The first thing that kindles ardor in learning is the greatness of the teacher. What is greater than the **Mother of God**? What more glorious than she whom glory itself chose?[88]

[87] Philip Schaff, *Nicene and Post-Nicene Fathers*, Series II, Vol. 7.
[88] Philip Schaff, *Nicene and Post-Nicene Fathers*, Series II, Vol. 10.

Chapter 9

A Great Cloud of Witnesses

Therefore, since we are surrounded
by so great a cloud of witnesses…
(Hebrews 12:1)

✞ What I **discovered** …

My Baptist church held weekly prayer services to pray on behalf of those in need. We established "prayer chains." Christian "prayer warriors" would offer intercessory prayer (e.g., "Oh, thanks for telling me about Sarah. We will add her to the prayer chain!"). But Protestant prayer chains are too small and should include the *entire* body of Christ, as we "are *one* body in Christ" (Romans 12:5). Brothers and sisters that have gone before us are *alive* in heaven and still part of the *one* Church. Therefore, they remain powerful prayer warriors in our prayer chain!

~ 📖 ~

Intercessory Prayer

Moses (a "prayer warrior") intercedes with God *on behalf of the people* to abstain from imposing His righteous judgment upon them. Notice how God hears Moses and answers his intercessory prayer:

> But Moses **implored the LORD**, his God, saying, "Why, O LORD, should your

> anger burn against **your people**, whom you brought out of the land of Egypt with great power and with a strong hand? Why should the Egyptians say, 'With evil intent he brought them out, that he might kill them in the mountains and wipe them off the face of the earth?' Turn from your burning wrath; change your mind about punishing your people. Remember your servants Abraham, Isaac, and Israel, and how you swore to them by your own self, saying, 'I will make your descendants as numerous as the stars in the sky; and all this land that I promised, I will give your descendants as their perpetual heritage.'" So the LORD changed his mind about the punishment he had threatened to inflict on his people (Exodus 32:11-14).

Praying to God, on behalf of someone else, is called *intercessory prayer*. Christians practice intercessory prayer every time we pray for someone or ask another person to pray for us.

Like the Old Testament, the New Testament is full of examples of intercessory prayer. Paul enthusiastically encourages Christians to pray to God *on behalf of others*:

> First of all, then, I ask that supplications, **prayers, petitions (intercessions)**, and thanksgivings be offered **for everyone**, for kings and all in authority, that we may lead

> a quiet and tranquil life, in all devotion and dignity (1 Timothy 2:1-2).

> He rescued us from such great danger of death, and He will continue to rescue us; in Him we have put our hope that He will also rescue us again, **as you help us with prayer**, so that thanks may be given by many on our behalf for the gift granted us **through the prayers of many** (2 Corinthians 1:10-11).

> …for I know that this will result in deliverance for me **through your prayers** and support from the Spirit of Jesus Christ (Philippians 1:19).

> With all **prayer and supplication**, pray at every opportunity in the Spirit. To that end, be watchful with all perseverance and **supplication for all the holy ones and also for me**, that speech may be given me to open my mouth, to make known with boldness the mystery of the gospel… (Ephesians 6:18-20).

Jesus *is* our One Mediator!

Paul teaches that Jesus is the one mediator between God and man:

> For there is one God, and there is **one mediator** between God and men, the man **Christ Jesus**, who gave Himself as a ransom

> for all, the testimony to which was given at the proper time (1 Timothy 2:5-6).

If intercession with God, on behalf of other people, denied that Christ is the one mediator between God and man, Paul was completely unaware of it.

> I urge you, brothers, by our Lord Jesus Christ and by the love of the Spirit, to *join* me in the struggle **by your prayers to God on my behalf**… (Romans 15:30-32).

Why didn't Paul, Peter, and early Christians go *directly* to God with their prayers?

Of course, Peter, Paul, and the early Christians *did* pray *directly* to God! However, they *also* asked for the prayers of others, as "this is good and pleasing to God our Savior" (1 Timothy 2:3). The early Church clearly practiced intercessory prayer! They did not believe intercessory prayer in any way interfered with Jesus as the *one* mediator.

***One* Body of Christ—Not *Two*!**

Christians are *one* family in Christ. We are *spiritually* united even through separation at death.

> I, then, a prisoner for the Lord, urge you to live in a manner worthy of the call you have received, with all humility and gentleness, with patience, bearing with one another through love, striving to preserve the unity of the spirit through the bond of peace: **one body and one Spirit**, as you were also

> called to the one hope of your call, **one Lord,** one faith, one baptism; one God and Father of all, who is over all and through all and in all (Ephesians 4:1-6).

The body of Christ, the Church,
is not one family on earth and a totally
different family in heaven!

> Rather, living the truth in love, we should grow in every way into Him who is the head, Christ, from whom the **whole body, joined and held together** by every supporting ligament, with the proper functioning of each part, brings about the body's growth and builds itself up in love (Ephesians 4:15-16).

Paul reminds us that we have different roles and gifts, but we remain *one* body in Christ. We have different parts, like a human body, but we are never torn apart to form two *different* bodies.

> For as in **one body** we have many parts, and all the parts do not have the same function, so we, though many, are **one body** in Christ and individually parts of one another (Romans 12:4-5).

> And let the peace of Christ control your hearts, the peace into which you were also called in **one body**. And be thankful (Colossians 3:15).

Not Even Death!

Death is unable to separate us from Christ. Death does not destroy the unity of the members of the *one* body of Christ, the Church. Jesus won the victory over death, so His Church would not be divided, broken by Satan, and unable to function.

> For I am convinced that neither **death**, nor life, nor angels, nor principalities, nor present things, nor future things, nor powers, nor height, nor depth, nor any other creature will be able to **separate us** from the love of God in Christ Jesus our Lord (Romans 8:38-39).

> And when this which is corruptible clothes itself with incorruptibility and this which is mortal clothes itself with immortality, then the word that is written shall come about: "Death is swallowed up in victory. Where, **O death is your victory**? Where, **O death is your sting?**" (1 Corinthians 15:54-55).

Communion of Saints

The *communion of saints* is a mystical and spiritual union between Christians living on earth and in heaven. Despite being physically separated, Christians on earth share prayer with our fellow brothers and sisters in heaven as *one* body of Christ. There is no Biblical evidence that the command to pray for one another suddenly ends when a Christian transitions from this life into heaven! The communion of saints involves the *entire* Christian family. Paul reminds us that we are all members of *one* household and held together by God:

> He came and preached peace to you who were far off and peace to those who were near, for through Him we both have access in **one** Spirit to the Father. So then you are no longer strangers and sojourners, but you are **fellow citizens with the holy ones** [note: saint = holy one, one set apart, one made holy] and **members of the household of God**, built upon the foundation of the apostles and prophets, with Christ Jesus Himself as the capstone. **Through Him** the whole structure is **held together** and grows into a temple sacred in the Lord; in Him you also are being built together into a dwelling place of God in the Spirit (Ephesians 2:17-22).

To reject the communion of saints is to, sadly, deny that Christians in heaven are still part of the Church!

Saints in Heaven Are Alive!

God is alive, His people are alive, and this is *not* dependent on their location! Apostolic Christians find any suggestion of praying to the *dead* entirely foreign to their faith. Indeed, the Catholic Church teaches that praying to the dead is incompatible with orthodox Christian faith. Saints are not dead; they are *alive* in heaven and standing in the very presence of God. The gift of intercessory prayer for each other includes all Christians in the *one* body of Christ.

James teaches that the "prayer of the righteous man" is powerful and effective (James 5:16). How much more powerful, then, are the prayers of the righteous in heaven who have been perfected in holiness?

The Communion of Saints is not a relationship between the living and the *dead*, but rather, the living and the *living* (Mark 12:27).

The Apostles' Creed

The Apostles' Creed is a very early statement of faith from the apostles. This creed, which predates the Nicene Creed, elegantly affirms that the first Christians believed in the "communion of saints"—so should we!

I believe in God
the Father almighty,
creator of heaven and earth.
I believe in Jesus Christ,
his only Son, our Lord.
He was conceived by the
power of the Holy Spirit
and born of the Virgin Mary.
He suffered under Pontius Pilate,
was crucified, died, and was buried.
He descended into hell.
On the third day he rose again.
He ascended into heaven
and is seated at the right hand of the Father.
He will come again to judge
the living and the dead.
I believe in the Holy Spirit,

the holy catholic Church,
the communion of saints,
the forgiveness of sins,
the resurrection of the body,
and the life everlasting.
Amen.

A Great Cloud of Witnesses

Hebrews records one of the most remarkable stories demonstrating the communion of saints. Those in the presence of God can see us. They are active witnesses in the mystical body of Christ! They have already run the race before them and are now cheering us on as a "great cloud of witnesses."

> Therefore, since **we are surrounded by so great a cloud of witnesses**, let us rid ourselves of every burden and sin that clings to us and persevere in running the race that lies before us while keeping our eyes fixed on Jesus, the leader and perfecter of faith… (Hebrews 12:1-2).

The Transfiguration

At the Transfiguration, Jesus took Peter, James, and John up to a mountain where they observed Elijah and Moses *talking* to Jesus. These Old Covenant saints, who died long ago, are *not* dead! Mark shows us that Christians continue to live in eternity. The mystical body of Christ is evident in this transformative interaction between heaven and earth:

> After six days, Jesus took Peter, James, and John and led them up a high mountain apart by themselves. And he was transfigured before them, and his clothes became dazzling white, such as no fuller on earth could bleach them. Then **Elijah** appeared to them along with **Moses**, and they were **conversing with Jesus**… (Mark 9:2-4).

Christian Martyrs Pray in Heaven

The prayers of Christian martyrs are described in Revelation. They demonstrate that those in heaven can, and do, pray! Martyrs are observed crying out to God for justice and they are reassured that their prayers will be answered:

> When he broke open the fifth seal, I saw **underneath the altar** the souls of those who had been **slaughtered because of the witness they bore to the word of God**. They cried out in a loud voice, "How long will it be, holy and true master, before you sit in judgment and avenge our blood on the inhabitants of the earth?" Each of them was given a white robe, and they were told to **be patient a little while longer** until the number was filled of their fellow servants and brothers who were going to be killed as they had been (Revelation 6:9-11).

Intercession of Angels

The Old Testament has multiple instances of incense being used in relation to worship. God instructed Moses to construct an altar of incense for worship (Exodus 30:1-10), which included how the incense was to be prepared (Exodus 30:34-38). In Psalms, incense is associated with the prayers of the saints:

> Let my **prayer** be counted as **incense** before you, and the lifting up of my hands as an evening sacrifice (Psalms 141:2).

Incense is also used in the New Testament. Recall the Magi brought gold, frankincense, and myrrh to worship Jesus (Matthew 2:10-11). John observed incense being used in his vision of the heavenly throne of God.

> Now when He had taken the scroll, the four living creatures and the twenty-four elders fell down before the Lamb, each having a harp, and golden **bowls full of incense**, which are the **prayers of the saints** (Revelation 5:8).

An angel intercedes by offering incense with the prayers of Christians:

> Another angel came and stood at the altar, holding a gold censer. He was given a great quantity of **incense** to offer, along with the **prayers of all the holy ones [saints],** on the gold altar that was before the throne. The smoke of the **incense** along with the **prayers of the holy ones** went up before

God from the hand of the angel (Revelation 8:3-4).

Honoring and Imitating Saints

Protestant Christianity teaches that *honoring* saints, for their various God-given virtues, distracts from worship that is due to God alone. Protestants suggest that *all* Christians are saints, to which, apostolic Christians faithfully agree! (Ephesians 1:1, 1 Corinthians 1:2, and Colossians 1:2). The Bible, however, also honors *certain* saints to point out virtues of faith that are helpful to our maturity in Christ. Hebrews highlights pillars of the faith that we are to *imitate*: by faith Abel, by faith Noah, by faith Abraham, by faith Moses, and so on (Hebrews 11). Hebrews continues: "Remember your leaders who spoke the word of God to you. Consider the outcome of their way of life and *imitate their faith*" (Hebrews 13:7). Surely, we would not charge the writer of Hebrews with taking honor away from Christ because he points out *certain individual saints* to be honored. The apostolic Church has followed this example of *honoring* virtuous saints. Christians find it helpful to read, understand, and *imitate* saints to orient their lives to sacrificially follow Christ. Paul himself encouraged Christians to follow his example or to *imitate* him: "Follow my example, as I follow the example of Christ" (1 Corinthians 11:1).

A young girl attended church with her grandfather one Sunday morning. The church had colorful stained-glass windows. The grandfather told his granddaughter that the windows were pictures of Saint Matthew, Saint Mark, Saint Luke, Saint John, and Saint Paul.

When she got home, the little girl told her mom and dad, with great excitement, what she had seen on these windows. Her dad asked, "What is a saint?" The girl thought for a moment and replied, "A saint is someone the light shines through." Saints are people who the "Son" shines through! We are the saints and Christ is the Light! Let the light of Christ shine through everything we do and shine on everyone we meet. Let's light up the world and become saints together!

There truly is a great "cloud of witnesses" surrounding us. We rejoice with the saints and ask them to "pray *with* us" and "pray *for* us," knowing they are part of our family. They root us on to the victory they themselves have obtained in Christ. For apostolic Christians, the communion of saints is a gift from God firmly established in the Bible. It is no wonder that the early Christian, Cyril of Jerusalem (AD 350), wrote:

> Then we commemorate also those who have fallen asleep before us, first Patriarchs, Prophets, Apostles, Martyrs, that at *their* prayers and *intercessions* God would receive *our* petition.[89]

[89] Philip Schaff, *Nicene and Post-Nicene Fathers*, Series II, Vol. 7.

Chapter 10

The Visual Gospel: The Crucifix, Sacred Icons, and Statues

But we proclaim Christ crucified!
(1 Corinthians 1:23)

✞ What I **discovered** …

The crucifix, sacred icons, and statues have been used since the time of Christ to *visually preach* the gospel. Many symbols (cross, stained-glass images, fish, shepherd, dove, praying hands, and Biblical scenes inside catacombs) are also used to prepare the Christian to enter into the presence of God. These visual gifts to the Church guide Christians into a deeper worship experience by recalling the Biblical truths they represent.

~ 📖 ~

"Don't you know He has risen?"

Why do most Christians have crucifixes in their Churches and homes? Don't they know Jesus has risen? To help answer this question, another question should be asked: Why did Paul preach Christ *crucified*? Doesn't Paul know that Jesus was raised from the dead? Certainly he does! Paul believes that through the crucified *and* resurrected Christ we have freedom from sin and death. Apostolic Christians follow this Biblical example by displaying both the crucifix *and* the cross.

The Crucifix—Salvation in Christ

In the First Book of Corinthians, Paul announces that his preaching arises from the *crucified* Christ!

> For Jews demand signs and Greeks look for wisdom, but **we proclaim Christ crucified**, a stumbling block to Jews and foolishness to Gentiles, but to those who are called, Jews and Greeks alike, Christ the power of God and the wisdom of God (1 Corinthians 1:22-24).

When Paul began speaking about his desire to reach the Corinthians for Christ, he did not come with eloquence or wisdom (1 Corinthians 2:1). What did he come proclaiming? Christ and Him *crucified*!

> O foolish Galatians! Who has bewitched you? Before your very **eyes** Jesus Christ was **publicly portrayed as crucified**? (Galatians 3:1).

What do our eyes see in this publicly portrayed crucified Christ? The parallel between this passage and the crucifix are self-apparent. The crucifix is an image not easily dismissed by the human mind and a powerful display of historical truth. Christians believe the crucifixion *and* the resurrection are both decisive events. These truths are to be shared with boldness, not reduced, hidden, or ignored. The fullness of the Gospel, despite being repulsive and hard to gaze upon, is an integral part of apostolic Christian faith. Catholic Christians and Orthodox Christians boldly portray the horrendous torture our Lord went through, so that we may be free from wrath.

> He Himself bore our sins in his **body** on the **cross**, so that, free from sins, we might live for righteousness; by his wounds **you have been healed** (1 Peter 2:24).

The Crucifix—Suffering for Christ

In some sects of Protestantism, a "health and wealth" gospel seems to prevail (name it and claim it preaching). In these Protestant traditions, *suffering* has no place in the life of the Christian. On the contrary, apostolic Christianity understands suffering much different. We are called to *sacrificially* follow Christ whether we are in good health and abundant prosperity, or, in poverty and painful suffering. When we *visually* observe the crucifix, we are reminded of the *Biblical reality* we are called to; which is a life of suffering. Ratzinger says:

> A worldview that is incapable of giving even pain meaning and value is good for nothing. It falls short precisely at the hour of the most serious crisis of existence. Those who have nothing to say about suffering except that we must fight against it are deceiving us. It is, of course, necessary to do everything one can to lessen the suffering of the innocent and to limit pain. But there is no human life without suffering, and he who is incapable of accepting suffering is refusing himself the purifications that alone allow us to reach maturity. In communion with Christ, pain becomes meaningful, not only for myself, as a process of *ablatio*

> in which God purges me of the dross that conceals his image, but beyond me, for the whole, so that we can all say with Saint Paul: "But now I rejoice in my *sufferings* for you and so complete in my flesh what is still lacking in the afflictions of Christ for the sake of his body, the Church" (Colossians 1:24).[90]

The crucifix calls to mind that suffering is a *unifying experience with Christ* as we "take up our cross" and follow Jesus (Matthew 16:24).

Christ suffered, was *crucified*, buried, and resurrected for our transgressions. Not everyone will be called to suffer in an extreme way, but when we suffer we surrender completely to Christ's mercy and grace. The crucifix is a reminder of our *unity* with Christ through whatever suffering we will endure in this life.

> ...but we also glory in our *sufferings*, because we know that *suffering* produces perseverance... (Romans 5:3).

Peter did not consider himself worthy to be crucified as Christ was, so he requested crucifixion upside down. Thomas, known as "doubting Thomas," was speared to death in India. John the Baptist was beheaded. Likewise, the Apostle Paul was beheaded. Christians are called to suffer, at times, and we should never forget the suffering that our Lord endured. Early Christians

---

[90] Joseph Cardinal Ratzinger, *Called to Communion* (San Francisco, CA: Ignatius Press, 1996), 155.

were willing to suffer and give their life for Christ. The crucifix is a *visual reminder* of this reality.

The Crucifixion *and* the Resurrection

Common objections to the crucifix are centered on the idea that, since Christ was resurrected from the dead, we should not display the crucified or suffering Christ. In this way, Protestant fundamentalism inadvertently pits the crucifixion against the resurrection. This interpretation leads to an "either/or" theology. Consequently, if one displays a crucifix, the assumption of neglecting the resurrection is silently assumed.

The apostolic Christian understanding is more complete based on a "both/and" theology. In other words, *both* the crucifixion *and* the resurrection of Christ are decisive and celebrated events in salvation history. Paul tells us that if Christ was not resurrected, our faith and hope are useless (1 Corinthians 15:17). This is precisely why Paul can say he was "*crucified* with Christ" (Galatians 2:19) and simultaneously proclaims a "living hope through the *resurrection* of Jesus Christ" (1 Peter 1:3).

> For Christians, the resurrection is the *single most important* event in history. It is precisely the resurrection that gives all people living hope!

Therefore, apostolic Christians humbly display *both* the cross and the crucifixion! We could never celebrate Resurrection Sunday without first having Good Friday! There is simply no crown without the cross! The empty Cross reminds us that we are to pick up our cross each day and follow Jesus (Matthew 16:24, Mark 8:34) and the crucifix is there to remind us of the price God paid for you and me!

The Visual Gospel

Icons are pictures used to express theological truths of the life, death, and resurrection of Jesus Christ. They guide our thoughts to spiritual truth in the same way written words on the pages of a Bible point us to truth. The sacred icon does not attempt to duplicate a person, event, or truth; rather, the icon represents a meaning. The truth is not an image; truth is Jesus Christ, God made flesh!

> Icons are not divine, but *point* to the Divine, by *visually preaching* the Gospel. Through the physical senses, icons guide us into a mystical and personal encounter with Jesus.

In the early Church, icons were used to *visually preach* the Gospel of Christ. Many people could not read. Texts were extremely expensive, making them unaffordable for common people. The early Church utilized icons to preach visual truth. These iconic "windows to the divine" have been used in Christian Church architecture for thousands of years. Icons guide us into a personal encounter, and mystical union, with Christ through our physical senses.

Sacred images speak "words" to the heart. In a similar manner, a word is a verbal "image." The Bishop of Rome (AD 590-604), Gregory the Great, explained it this way:

> For what writing presents to readers, this a picture presents to the unlearned...since in it even the ignorant see what they ought to follow; in it the illiterate read.[91]

The reflection and contemplation that arise from the visual Gospel is another form of evangelism through liturgical art. Professor John Vidmar writes that John of Damascus affirmed the divine usefulness of icons and pictures. He states:

> The Gospels, he wrote, were verbal accounts of the Lord's words and actions, while icons were pictorial accounts; reject the latter and you are in danger of rejecting the former, because their content is identical. Finally, much as the Gospels were shown public respect (standing, bowing, processing, holding candles to either side, incensing, etc.), so too icons deserved similar public honor.[92]

Think About It!

If you are like my family, you have either read or have children's books with pictures depicting Moses, Abraham, Noah, Peter, and Mary. These *images* of Jesus illustrate how He miraculously walked on water, healed the sick, calmed storms, entered Jerusalem on a donkey, taught the disciples, cleansed the lepers, and

---

[91] Philip Schaff, *Nicene and Post-Nicene Fathers*, Series II, Vol. 13.

[92] John Vidmar, *The Catholic Church Through the Ages: A History* (Mahwah, NJ: Paulist Press, 2014), 107.

told Zacchaeus to come down from the tree—among other Biblical truths. These books have colorful *images* representing Jesus being crucified, buried, and resurrected. Would anyone claim these illustrations and images in children's books are graven images?

An icon is worth a thousand sermons!

Apostolic Christians use icons, pictures, and statues as reminders of heroes of the faith. This is no different than pictures and statues of great heroes in the Sports Hall of Fame. Like the heroes remembered, they encourage us to accomplish great things, so too, images and icons encourage Christians to grow closer to Christ!

We display pictures of family around our home which are reminders of their life and love we hold dear. In the Church, pictures and images are intended to bring a *visual* picture of the Gospel. Apostolic Christians pray in the presence of these sacred icons but *do not* worship the image. We can understand, by these examples, not all images equate to graven images. The apostolic Church simply uses icons to point us beyond the physical to the spiritual.

God Is Not Limited

In evangelical fundamentalism, the spiritual and physical are sometimes held in opposition as though God only works through the spiritual. However, the Bible is filled with examples showing God working through physical and material objects to accomplish His work. Do we truly believe that God used a bronze serpent to heal people bitten by snakes? (Numbers

21:9). Do we believe that the sick were really healed by the passing of a shadow from Peter? (Acts of the Apostles 5:15). Do we believe that aprons and handkerchiefs touched by Paul actually healed and drove out demons? (Acts of the Apostles 19:11-12). What about the physical bones of saints? Do we believe God used the bones of Elisha to resurrect a dead man (2 Kings 13:21) or that Jesus used clay and His saliva to heal a blind man? (John 9:6-7). Christians believe God did, and still does today, work through the physical world to accomplish spiritual works of salvation.

The Early Church on Sacred Icons

During the eighth century, a controversy arose between *iconoclasts* and *iconodules.* The iconoclasts believed religious icons should be completely destroyed. Yet, icondules believed that sacred images should be revered within the Church. The Seventh Ecumenical Council of the Church was held in AD 787, which affirmed that sacred icons should not be worshipped; however, icons were encouraged to be revered and used within the Church to preach Jesus Christ. From this Church council, we read this positive affirmation: "The honor which is paid to the image passes on to that which the image represents."

Images for a Divine Purpose

When God provided instructions to Moses concerning the Tabernacle, He commanded that the sheets have images of cherubim woven into them:

> The tabernacle itself you shall make out of ten sheets woven of fine linen twined and of violet, purple, and scarlet yarn, with **cherubim embroidered on them** (Exodus 26:1).

Images of palm trees and flowers were used to decorate the temple. Carved cherubim were made in the walls, with floors made of pure gold (1 Kings 6:23-36).

Statues

Christians are not to make graven images or bow down to idols (Deuteronomy 4:16-18, Leviticus 26:1). Consider what God said in Exodus:

> You **shall not** make for yourself an **idol** or a likeness of anything in the heavens above or on the earth below or in the waters beneath the earth; you shall **not bow down** before them or serve them (Exodus 20:4-5).

Protestant, Orthodox, and Catholic Christians all agree! Yet, God did not forbid the religious *use* of statues. At the same time God forbade the worship of idols, just a few chapters later He *commanded* His people to build two golden statues. These statues were to be placed on the Ark of the Covenant!

> You shall then make a cover of pure gold, two and a half cubits long, and one and a half cubits wide. **Make two cherubim of beaten gold** for the two ends of the cover; make one cherub at one end, and the other at the other end, of one piece with the cover, at each end… (Exodus 25:17-19).

The Ark of the Covenant holding the Commandments, which Bible fundamentalists contend prohibit all images, is actually covered with sacred images itself!

In the Book of Numbers, a bronze statue was also created at the command of God. Moses made these statues for a divine purpose. God used a bronze serpent to bring healing to the people:

> Then the people came to Moses and said, "We have sinned in complaining against the LORD and you. Pray to the LORD to take the serpents from us." So Moses prayed for the people, and the LORD said to Moses: **Make a seraph** and **mount it on a pole** and everyone who has been bitten will look at it and recover. Accordingly **Moses made a bronze serpent** and mounted it on a pole, and whenever the serpent bit someone, the person looked at the bronze serpent and recovered (Numbers 21:7-9).

It was not the bronze material but God's power working through the physical world that brought healing and accomplished His purpose. In the First Book of Kings, two wooden statues were built. Where were they placed? *In the sanctuary*!

> In the inner sanctuary he **made two cherubim**, each ten cubits high, **made of pine**... He **placed the cherubim in the inmost part of the house**... He **overlaid**

> **the cherubim with gold** (1 Kings 6:23-28).

A Protestant study Bible explains these cherubim were "made of olive wood and overlaid…with gold. Standing like sentries facing the door (2 Chronicles 3:13), their combined wingspan reached from wall to wall. Along with the two smaller *cherubim* facing each other atop the Ark (Exodus 25:17-21), they *symbolized* the awesome presence of the Most Holy God."[93] Similar to how these cherubim represented God's presence, apostolic Christians use statues and sacred icons as visual reminders of the *same* powerful truth. Statues help Christians recall Biblical truth, people, or events.

Consider this: The Lincoln Memorial in Washington D.C. was built in honor of Abraham Lincoln. Millions of people pass before the statue and observe the history and importance of this president. These people *honor* Abraham Lincoln, but not a single person would claim to be worshipping the physical statue.

At many other places in D.C., you find statues and images of Americans that have served this country. They are honored for their virtuous character. For statues of early Christian martyrs and saints, how great is it to likewise honor them for being Christ-like? The visual nature of these statues is also a great example for our youth.

During the Advent and Christmas seasons, nativity scenes using statues of Mary, Joseph, baby Jesus, and the wise men are placed on the lawns of churches

---

[93] *NLT Study Bible*, 2nd Edition (Carol Stream, IL: Tyndale House Publishers, 2008), 584.

and homes to announce the birth of Christ. Catholic Churches have more permanent statues for the *same purpose.* The only difference is that they display statues year round, while some Protestant Christians restrict displaying statues to only Advent and Christmas.

Catholics *honor* what statues *represent*,
but they are never worshipped!

Protestant Churches Have Statues and Icons, Too!

Many evangelical churches have statues, icons, and other visual reminders of faith.

Protestant mega-church (Houston, Texas): In this evangelical church, there is a large, golden, rotating globe on stage. Apparently, this globe is to *visually* remind the congregation that Christians are to reach the entire "world" with the Gospel of Jesus Christ.[94]

United Methodist church (Houston, Texas): Outside the St. Paul's United Methodist Church, sits a large statue of Christ. The church website describes the statue's artistic and spiritual value: "Outside, the statue of Christ that stands on the south lawn of the church was given by the Henderson family. The statue has drawn people to it for four decades, and it is not unusual to see individuals sitting on benches near it gazing up into the face of Jesus."[95]

---

[94] Joel Osteen Ministries, Houston, TX. https://www.joelosteen.com.

[95] St. Paul's United Methodist Church, Houston, TX. http://www.stpaulshouston.org/.

Lutheran church (St. Louis, Missouri): At the Historic Trinity Lutheran Church, front and center of the congregation, there is a life-size statue of Jesus looking down on the altar.[96]

Lutheran church (Milwaukee, Wisconsin): Our Savior's Lutheran Church, member of the Evangelical Lutheran Church in America (ELCA), has multiple iconic stained-glass images of Christ and a life-size statue of Jesus at the front entrance of the church.[97]

First Baptist church (Huntsville, Alabama): This church has a very beautiful mosaic of Christ. The church says, "The mosaic was designed to express the Biblical theme, 'Creation and Redemption.' Revelation 1:12-20 serves as the primary Biblical text inspiring the design."[98]

Episcopal church (Philadelphia, Pennsylvania): St. Luke's Episcopal Church has a crucifix statue on the lawn, in addition to iconic imagery and pictures in the ceiling of the sanctuary. This Episcopal church describes the worship in this way: "…you will hear chanting and bells ringing, you will see movement and color among the ministers and their vestments, and you will smell incense. In Anglo-Catholic services, all the worshipper's senses are utilized and all means at our disposal are employed to 'worship the Lord in the beauty of holiness' (Ps. 96:9). You will

---

[96] Historic Trinity Lutheran Church, St. Louis, MO. http://www.trinitystlouis.com/.

[97] Our Savior's Lutheran Church, Milwaukee, WI. http://www.oslcmilw.org/.

[98] First Baptist, Huntsville, AL. http://www.fbchsv.org/.

also notice some bowing, standing, and kneeling by the clergy or members of the congregation—these are ways in which we show our reverence for the holiness of God."[99]

Presbyterian church (Lockport, New York): This Presbyterian church has beautiful stained-glass images lining the sanctuary. Biblical and religious iconic themes, including images of Jesus, Mary, Joseph, and angels are represented as treasures of the church.[100]

Thousands of examples of Protestant churches having icons or statues could be added to this list. What conclusion can be drawn from this? I do not believe that our brothers and sisters in Christ within Baptist, Methodist, Episcopal, Lutheran, or non-denominational traditions are worshipping any of these statues! Nor, would I suggest that these religious icons or stained-glass windows lead to idolatry.

Like these evangelical Protestant traditions, the apostolic Church has visual reminders of the glorious Gospel!

[99] St. Luke's Episcopalian Church, Philadelphia, PA. http://www.stlukesger.org/about.html.

[100] First Presbyterian Church, Lockport, NY. http://1stpreslockport.org/.

Chapter 11

Entering Into His Presence

Let everything that has breath praise the Lord.
(Psalms 150:6)

✞ What I **discovered** …

The Mass is precisely where Christians gather to experience God as *one* body of Christ. We were never created to be spectators. Rather, we are invited to *actively participate* in glorifying God through partaking in the literal body and blood of Jesus. Through the Holy Spirit, by faith, and our physical senses, we are ushered into the heavenly realm and mystically united with Christ. Blessed are those who are invited to the Supper of the Lamb!

A Walk Through the Christian Mass!

We begin by sealing ourselves with a public proclamation declaring that we belong to God by making the Sign of the Cross—an ancient practice and visible sign. We proclaim, in unity, "…in the name of the Father, and of the Son, and of the Holy Spirit" (Matthew 28:19). The Sign of the Cross is a mark of surrender to our King Jesus, a confession of His crucifixion, suffering, death, and resurrection. It is a reminder of God's love for us and that we are to deny ourselves and follow

Him. Jesus is the very center of our life and the Sign of the Cross is a personal act of faith made public.

> The most basic Christian gesture in prayer is and always will be the sign of the Cross. It is a way of confessing Christ crucified with one's very body, in accordance with the programmatic words of St. Paul: "We preach Christ Crucified…" Again he says: "I decided to know nothing among you except Jesus Christ and Him crucified" (1 Corinthians 2:2). To seal oneself with the sign of the Cross is a visible and public Yes to Him who suffered for us… The sign of the Cross is a confession of faith: I believe in Him who suffered for me and rose again; in Him who has transformed the sign of shame into a sign of hope and of the love of God that is present with us… By signing ourselves with the Cross, we place ourselves under the protection of the Cross, hold it in front of us like a shield that will guard us in all the distress of daily life and give us the courage to go on. We accept it as a signpost that we follow: "If any man come after me, let him deny himself and take up his cross and follow me" (Mark 8:34). The Cross shows us the road of life—the imitation of Christ. We connect the sign of the Cross with confession of faith in the triune God—the Father, the Son, and the Holy Spirit. In this way it becomes a remembrance of

Baptism, which is particularly clear when we use holy water with it.[101]

We physically kneel to acknowledge the holy presence of God, our Heavenly Father, and King. The Biblical act of kneeling was practiced by Peter, Paul, and the early Christians. Peter "...got down on his *knees* and prayed" (Acts of the Apostles 9:40). Paul said, "For this reason I *kneel* before the Father..." (Ephesians 3:14-15). Do we not believe that "at the name of Jesus *every knee should bow*, in heaven and on earth and under the earth, and every tongue confess that Jesus Christ is Lord, to the glory of God the Father?" (Philippians 2:10-11). Surely, He is worthy! Christians believe and follow this truth to the physical limit.

We are greeted with "The Lord be with you!" as we return the words "And with your spirit!" As the priest blesses us and asks for God to shower us with His Spirit, so too, we lift up the priest. In Scripture, we find this greeting many places: "The Lord be with your spirit. Grace be with you" (2 Timothy 4:22), "May the grace of the LORD Jesus Christ, and the love of God, and the fellowship of the Holy Spirit be with you all" (2 Corinthians 13:14), "Grace and peace to you from God our Father and the LORD Jesus Christ" (Philippians 1:2), and "Grace and peace to you from God our Father and the LORD Jesus Christ" (Ephesians 1:2).

As an act of public confession, with the entire body of Christ, we acknowledge our sins and faults as *one* body. Notice the direct Biblical references within this

---

[101] Joseph Cardinal Ratzinger, *The Spirit of the Liturgy* (San Francisco, CA: Ignatius Press, 2000), 177-178.

verbal confession: "If we *acknowledge* our sins, he is faithful and just and will forgive our sins and cleanse us from every wrongdoing" (1 John 1:9). "Therefore, *confess* your sins to *one another*..." (James 5:16). As a visual sign of acknowledging our sin, we physically strike our breast to show accountability for our sin, precisely as the early Christians did: "The tax collector stood at a distance. He would not even look up to heaven, but beat his breast and said, *God have mercy on me a sinner*" (Luke 18:13).

> I confess to almighty God, and to you, my brothers and sisters, that I have greatly sinned in my thoughts and in my words, in what I have done and in what I have failed to do, through my fault, through my fault, through my most grievous fault. Therefore, I ask blessed Mary ever-Virgin, all the Angels and Saints, and you, my brothers and sisters, to pray for me to the Lord our God.

We ask for God's limitless mercy on our life, by proclaiming: "Lord, have mercy," an echo found in the Gospels: "...God, be merciful to me a sinner...have mercy on me...have mercy on me!" (Luke 18:13, 38, 39).

We then sing an ancient hymn of praise proclaiming glory to God in the highest, and on earth peace to people of good will, which echoes the angelic praise when Jesus was born: "Glory to God in the highest, and on earth peace to men of good will" (Luke 2:14).

We publicly thank God for the proclaimed word of the Lord saying, "Thanks be to God." The model for our praise is directly from the Bible: "*...the word of the Lord* abides forever" (1 Peter 1:25). "*Thanks be to God* through Jesus Christ our Lord..." (Romans 7:25).

Next is the Liturgy of the Word. We listen to the first reading which comes from the Old Testament, followed by a responsorial psalm. The second reading is taken from one of the New Testament letters. Then, we join in unity as we stand together and prepare to hear the Gospel proclaimed. We make the Sign of the Cross over our forehead, mouth, and heart. This confession asks God to always have the Gospel in our mind, on our lips, and within our heart! The priest gives a homily with Biblical application for our daily lives.

As *one* body of Christ, we stand united and proclaim the same profession of faith that the early Christians professed: The Nicene Creed, a confession of ancient Christian orthodoxy! We join with ancient voices to proclaim our universal faith. We follow the Traditions passed down to us from the apostles.

In the Eucharistic prayer, we hear praise and exhortation: "Holy, Holy, Holy, Lord God of hosts" which is derived directly from Scripture: "... never cease to sing, 'Holy, Holy, Holy is the Lord God Almighty, who was and is and is to come'" (Revelation 4:8) and "Holy, Holy, Holy..." (Isaiah 6:3).

The words at the Last Supper are recalled: "Take this, all of you, and eat of it, for this is my body, which will be given up for you... Take this, all of you, and drink from it, for this is the chalice of my blood, the blood of the New and Eternal Covenant, which will be poured out for you and for many for the forgiveness of sins. *Do this* in memory of me."

"Take, eat; this is my body"
(Matthew 26:26, Mark 14:22)

"Drink of it, all of you, for this is my blood of
the covenant…"
(Matthew 26:27-28)

"This chalice which is poured out for you is the new
covenant in my blood"
(Luke 22:20)

"blood of the eternal covenant"
(Hebrew 13:20)

"…which is poured out for many"
(Mark 14:24)

"This chalice is the new covenant in my blood. Do
this, as often as you drink it, in remembrance of me."
(1 Corinthians 11:25, Luke 22:19)

As a memorial of the death of our Lord, we hear: "We proclaim your Death, O Lord, and profess your Resurrection until you come again." This too is taken from Holy Scripture (which in turn, adapted it from the ancient liturgy of the Mass since it was celebrated years before these words were written down): "For as often as you eat this bread and drink the chalice, you proclaim the death of the Lord until he comes" (1 Corinthians 11:26).

Angels in heaven unite with us as we move expectantly into the throne room of God in the Mass. This is a time heaven meets earth, and earth meets heaven. We are not alone! The intercession of the saints unites our entire Christian family. We are in the company of a great cloud of witnesses (Hebrews 12:1) whom we ask for prayers and intercession, as they are alive and part of the *one* body of Christ.

> We are invited into the throne room of heaven for an hour each Sunday to worship alongside the angels. We are being ushered into the upper room of Holy Thursday to recline at the Lord's Table. We are on the mount of Calvary as our Lord offers Himself to the Father on our behalf. Make no mistake: The Mass is not about God "reaching down" to earth as much as it is about us being swept up into heaven.[102]

As a family in Christ, we stand united and pray our Lord's Prayer as Jesus taught us:

> Our Father, who art in heaven,
> hallowed be thy name;
> thy kingdom come;
> thy will be done
> on earth as it is in heaven.
> Give us this day our daily bread;
> and forgive us our trespasses
> as we forgive those who trespass against us;
> and lead us not into temptation,
> but deliver us from evil. Amen.
> (Matthew 6:9-13)

The body of Christ then offers each other the sign of peace, "Peace be with you." This too is taken directly

---

[102] Mark Hart, *Behold the Mystery* (Frederick, MD: The Word Among Us Press, 2014), 13.

from the Bible: "...peace be with you" (John 20:19), "Peace be with you..." (John 20:21), and "Now the God of peace be with you all. Amen" (Romans 15:33).

In preparation for Holy Communion, we hear "Lamb of God" multiple times, taken from when John was out baptizing: "Behold, the Lamb of God who takes away the sin of the world!" (John 1:29).

We take to heart, and verbally proclaim, the words taken directly from the story of the Roman centurion before taking Holy Communion. To be sure, we are not worthy, as we recite:

> "Lord, I am not worthy that you should enter under my roof, but only say the word and my soul shall be healed" (Matthew 8:8).

The Center of Worship—Jesus!

In the *Christ*-centric Mass, we stand at the foot of the Cross and receive the Body, Blood, Soul, and Divinity of our Lord through the Sacrament of the Holy Eucharist. We gather not for the pastor, the music, or even a sermon! Rather, we gather together to partake in the mystical Eucharist that our Lord instituted 2,000 years ago on the night He was betrayed. This is the mystery of the faith!

As Christians, we are called to the Lord's Supper and receive through faith the Eucharist. This celebration unites believers until Christ returns. Jesus told the disciples, and us, to "do this" in a perpetual way. The Real Presence of Christ is *not* a symbol. Rather, it is His *real* body and *real* blood poured out for us! The mystical reality performed through the Holy Spirit brings

Christ to us. We are participants, partakers, and family at a feast through the Sacrament of the Eucharist.

> At the heart of the Eucharistic celebration are the bread and wine that, by the words of Christ and the invocation of the Holy Spirit, become Christ's Body and Blood. Faithful to the Lord's command the Church continues to do, in his memory and until his glorious return, what he did on the eve of his Passion: "He took bread. . . ." "He took the cup filled with wine. . . ." The signs of bread and wine become, in a way surpassing understanding, the Body and Blood of Christ...[103]

Jesus said, "He who eats *my flesh* and drinks *my blood* abides in me, and I in him" (John 6:56). Apostolic Christianity is founded on Christ and we remain in Him by partaking in the Eucharist.

After hearing the Liturgy of the Word, and experiencing the Liturgy of the Eucharist, the body of Christ is challenged with these beautiful words: "Go, and announce the Gospel of the Lord." These words echo our Lord's great commission to all Christians:

> Therefore, go and make disciples of all nations, baptizing them in the name of the Father, and of the Son, and of the Holy Spirit, and teaching them to obey everything I have commanded you. And surely I am with you always, to the very end of the age (Matthew 28:19-20).

[103] CCC, n. 1333

Prayer for the Unity of *All* Christians

O God, the Father of our Lord Jesus Christ, our only Savior, the Prince of Peace, give us the courage to consider seriously the great dangers we, as Christians, are in by our many unfortunate divisions. Deliver us from all hatred and prejudice and whatever else may hinder us from union and concord. There is but one body and one spirit, and one hope of our calling, one Lord, one faith, one baptism, one God and Father of us all. So may we all be of one heart and one soul, united in the holy bonds of truth and peace, of faith and love. May we glorify You with one mind and one voice. We ask this through Christ our Lord. Amen.

About Leonine Publishers

Leonine Publishers LLC makes fine Catholic literature available to Catholics throughout the English-speaking world. Leonine Publishers offers an innovative "hybrid" approach to book publication that helps authors as well as readers. Please visit our web site at www.leoninepublishers.com to learn more about us. Browse our online bookstore to find more solid Catholic titles to uplift, challenge, and inspire.

Our patron and namesake is Pope Leo XIII, a prudent, yet uncompromising pope during the stormy years at the close of the 19th century. Please join us as we ask his intercession for our family of readers and authors.

Do you have a book inside you? Visit our web site today. Leonine Publishers accepts manuscripts from Catholic authors like you. If your book is selected for publication, you will have an active part in the production process. This book is an example of our growing selection of literature for the busy Catholic reader of the 21st century.

www.leoninepublishers.com

CPSIA information can be obtained
at www.ICGtesting.com
Printed in the USA
FFOW05n1141281117

9 781942 190394